STATE OF THE ART PROGRAM

Portfolios

Robyn Montana Turner

Educating tomorrow today

BARRETT KENDALL PUBLISHING, Ltd.

AUSTIN, TEXAS

CREDITS

EDITORIAL

Project Director: *Linda Dunlap*

Senior Development Editor: *Linda Dunlap*

Editors: *Melissa Blackwell Burke, Claire Miller Colombo, Kathleen Fitzgibbon, Jody Frank, Mary Ann Frishman, Patty Moynahan, Tara Turner, Anne Walker*

Copy Editors: *Kathleen Unger, Sandra Wolfgang*

Editorial Support: *Mary Corbett, Elaine Clift Gore, Judy McBurney*

Administrative Manager: *Mark Blangger*

Administrative Support: *Laurie O'Meara*

DESIGN, PRODUCTION, AND PHOTO RESEARCH

Project Director: *Pun Nio*

Designers: *Leslie Kell Designs, Jane Thurmond Designs, Pun Nio*

Design and Electronic Files: *Dodson Publication Services, Leslie Kell Designs, Jane Thurmond Designs, Linda Kensicki*

Photo Research: *Mark Blangger, Laurie O'Meara*

Photo Art Direction: *Jodie Baker, Andrew Yates Photography*

Cover Design: *Leslie Kell Designs; Art Director, Pun Nio; Student Art: Bus-Wendy, Gunther, Patrick, Lucia, and Stacy, Langford Elementary; Face-Luis, Allison Elementary; Sun-Katie, Woodridge Elementary; Star-Alicia, Woodridge Elementary; Palm Tree-Lisa, Eanes Elementary; Baboon-Su Jin, Hill Elementary; Leaves-Lakela, Amelia Earhart Learning Center; Tin Man-Elena, Cambridge Elementary; Background-Brushworks Photo Disc.*

Printed in the United States of America

ISBN 1-889105-14-7   3 4 5 6 7   VH 02 01 00 99 98

STATE OF THE ART PROGRAM

Portfolios

CONSULTANTS

Doug Blandy, Ph.D.
Associate Professor
  Program in Arts and Administration
  University of Oregon
  Eugene, Oregon

Cindy G. Broderick, Ph.D.
Art Faculty
  Alamo Heights Junior School
  Alamo Heights Independent
    School District
  San Antonio, Texas

Sara Chapman, M.A.
Visual Arts Coordinator
  Alief Independent School District
  Houston, Texas

Brenda J. Chappell, Ph.D.
Art Consultant
  University of Tennessee
  Nashville, Tennessee

James Clarke, M.A.
*Program Director for Visual Arts and
Elementary Creative Drama*
  Aldine Independent School District
  Houston, Texas

Georgia Collins, Ph.D.
Professor, Department of Art
  University of Kentucky
  Lexington, Kentucky

Gloria Contreras, Ph.D.
*Professor, Department of Teacher
Education and Administration*
  University of North Texas
  Denton, Texas

Sandra M. Epps, Ph.D.
Director, Multicultural Programs
  Community School District Five
  New York, New York

Diane C. Gregory, Ph.D.
*Associate Professor of Art Education,
Department of Art and Design*
  Southwest Texas State University
  San Marcos, Texas

Susan M. Mayer, M.A.
*Coordinator of Museum Education,
Senior Lecturer of Art*
  The University of Texas at Austin
  Austin, Texas

Aaronetta Hamilton Pierce
Consultant
  African American Art and Artists
  San Antonio, Texas

Renee Sandell, Ph.D.
Professor, Department of Art Education
  Maryland Institute, College of Art
  Baltimore, Maryland

iii

CONTRIBUTING WRITERS

Pamela Geiger Stephens, Ph.D.
Art Education Consultant
Colleyville, Texas

Sharon Warwick, M. Ed., M.S.A.
Art Specialist
Central Junior High School
Euless, Texas
Tarrant County Junior College
Hurst, Texas

Kay K. Wilson, M.A.
Art Specialist
North Texas Institute for Educators
on the Visual Arts
University of North Texas
Denton, Texas

REVIEWERS

Gini Robertson-Baker
Classroom Teacher
Bivins Elementary School
Amarillo Independent School District
Amarillo, Texas

Rosalinda Champion
Art Specialist
Edinburg Senior High School
Edinburg Consolidated School District
Edinburg, Texas

Kathleen Donner
Art Specialist
Chatsworth High School
Los Angeles Unified School District
Chatsworth, California

Nancy Mayeda
Principal, Creative Fine Arts
Magnet School
San Francisco Unified School District
San Francisco, California

Suzanne Pfenninger
Classroom Teacher
Lowell Elementary School
Warren County Public School District
Indianapolis, Indiana

Betty Rosenbaum
Classroom Teacher
Abingdon Elementary School
Washington County Schools
Abingdon, Virginia

Sharon St. Clair
Art Specialist
Walt Disney Elementary School
Magnolia Elementary School District
Anaheim, California

Jack Tovey
Art Specialist
Bear Creek Elementary School
Pinellas County Schools
St. Petersburg, Florida

Marilyn Wylie
Art Specialist
Bethune Academy
Aldine Independent School District
Houston, Texas

CONTENTS

v

Georges Seurat. (Detail) *A Sunday on La Grande Jatte – 1884*, 1884–1886. Oil on canvas, 83 by 123¼ inches. Helen Birch Bartlett Memorial Collection, 1926.224. Photograph © 1996, The Art Institute of Chicago. All rights reserved.

Art All Around

You are an artist. Ideas for art are all around you. What do you see when you look at art?

Artists create artworks in many ways. They use **elements of art** in fresh and original ways. The elements of art are line, shape, color, value, texture, form, and space.

Artists plan how the elements will work together in an artwork. They use **principles of design** as guides for their plans. The principles of design are unity, variety, emphasis, balance, pattern, rhythm, and proportion. You will learn more about some of the elements of art and principles of design in this unit.

First Look

Where does this artwork probably take place? Does it take place today or long ago? Explain. How do you think the people in it feel?

Seeing Like an Artist

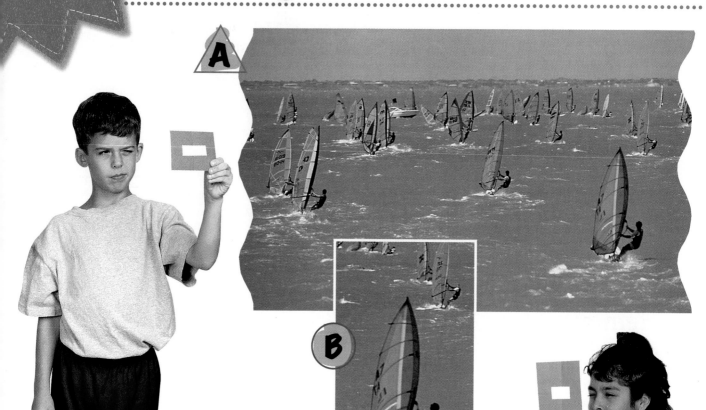

Artists like to study the world around them. They look for different designs. They train their eyes, to notice **details,** or small parts, of a **design.**

Look at all the pictures on these pages. Picture **B** is a detail of **A**. Picture **C** is a detail, too. How can you tell?

C Grace, Smith Elementary. *Bike Shadows*. Watercolor, crayon, 18 by 12 inches.

How to
Make a Detail Detector

Which details might be hidden away in this book?
Which types of details might you find in your classroom?

1. Fold a paper evenly one way and then the other way.

2. Cut a straight line to make a triangle where the folds meet.

3. Open your Detail Detector and place it on a design. Move it around.

4. Become a Detail Detective to find more interesting details.

Seeing, Planning, Thinking Like an Artist

You can train your eye to see details everywhere.
Begin by making a Detail Detector.
Use it to find details of pictures in this unit.
Then find some interesting details in your classroom.
Make a list describing five of the most interesting details.
Compare your list with your friends' lists.

Alma Gunter. *Dinner on Grounds*, 1979–80. Acrylic on canvas, 24 by 18 inches. Billy R. Allen Folk Art Collection. African American Museum, Dallas, Texas. Gift of Mr. and Mrs. Robert Decherd.

Community Gatherings

People who share common interests and live nearby form a community. They often gather together for community events. What are some community events you've attended?

Look at **A**. What is going on in the artwork? What kinds of **lines** do you see? With your finger in the air, make some of the lines you see in **B**. Artists use different types of **media**. Some media are pencil, paint, chalk, crayon, marker, clay, and computer.

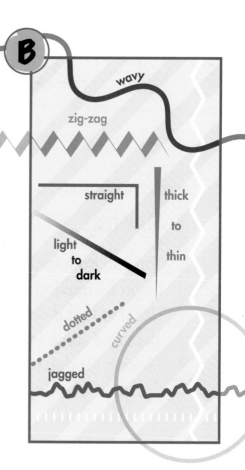

wavy

zig-zag

straight

thick

to

thin

light

to

dark

dotted

curved

jagged

Lesson 1

Miguel Vivancos, *Village Feast*, 1951. Oil on canvas, approximately 22½ by 29¼ inches. Musée National d'Art Moderne, Centre Georges Pompidou, Paris.

Lines can be **edges** of **shapes.** Some **geometric** shapes are triangles, circles, and rectangles. Point to some of these in **A** and **C.** Can you find **organic** shapes such as leaves, clothing, or animals?

Toby, Zavala Elementary. *The Apartment.* Marker on paper, 12 by 9 inches.

 Try Your Hand
Drawing from Memory
1. Draw a picture of a community event that you remember.
2. Use your crayons or markers.
3. Show who came and what happened.

Planning Like an Artist

The pictures in **A**, **B**, **C**, and **D** show things happening quickly. Even so, the artists planned them carefully. They showed **motion** with lines and shapes. Point to things that show motion in the pictures.

Many artists plan before they create artworks. Often they plan by making **sketches.** Their sketches help them remember what they've seen.

Warren, Brauchle Elementary. *Fantastic Bird.* Tempera, marker on paper, 18 by 12 inches.

How to
Make a Sketchbook

1. Fold eight sheets of drawing paper in halves. Staple on the fold.

2. Cast the shadow of your face to be about the size of your book. Ask a friend to draw around your silhouette.

3. Cut out your silhouette. Draw around it on colored construction paper. Then cut that out.

4. Glue your silhouette onto your book. Decorate it to be especially like you.

What title will you give your sketchbook?
How can your friends tell that it's yours?

Some artists like to draw their sketches in a **sketchbook.** How do you suppose a sketchbook helps artists plan and learn?

Artists make sketches about many types of **subjects.** An artwork can be about animals, people, places, and things.

What subjects do you like to draw? Tell about some of the sketches you've made.

Seeing, Planning, Thinking Like an Artist

Make a sketchbook to help you plan and learn. Which subjects will you draw first?

Henri Rousseau. *Le joueurs de football (The Football Players)*, 1908. Oil on canvas, 39½ by 31⅝ inches. The Solomon R. Guggenheim Museum, New York. © The Solomon R. Guggenheim Foundation, New York (FN 60.1583). Photograph by David Heald.

Community Games

Community sports bring people together to play. What are some of your favorite games? Do you play them in your community? Explain.

What is happening in **A** and **B**? How did the artists create motion in each picture?

What do you notice first in **A**? A ball is the **center of interest.** The artist used **emphasis** to lead your eye to the ball.

Pieter Brueghel, the Elder. *Children's Games*, 1560. Oil on oakwood, 47 by 64 inches. Kunsthistorisches Museum, Vienna, Austria. Photograph by Erich Lessing/ Art Resource, New York.

Some artworks do not have a center of interest. The artist of **B** showed many kinds of games in a painting made long ago. Count the games being played in **B**.

Compare **A** and **B**. What is the subject of both paintings? Point to a game you would like to play.

Crystal, Zavala Elementary. *Having Fun Fishing*, Pages in a flipbook. Index cards, colored pencil, 4 by 6 inches.

Try Your Hand
Making a Flipbook
Make a flipbook to show something in motion. Will the drawings in your flipbook have a center of interest?
1. Draw the beginning and ending stages on two index cards.
2. Draw the middle stage on another index card.
3. Draw the other two stages on two more index cards.
4. Hold the five index cards with one hand and flip them with the other.
5. Make a cover with another index card.
How can you make your flipbook work backwards?

Planning Like an Artist 9

Thinking Like an Artist

You probably think like an artist every day. Do you usually wear two shoes instead of just one? Did you brush your top and bottom teeth today? Have you ridden a bicycle lately? If so, you're thinking about **balance.** Artists think about balance when they create artworks.

Picture **A** shows **symmetrical balance.** The right and left sides are about the same. Which things around you show **symmetry**?

How does it feel to pet a kitten? Why are new cars shiny? To answer these questions, you must think about **texture.** Artists think about texture when they create artworks.

 D James Wyeth. *Portrait of Pig*, 1970. Oil on canvas, 51½ by 83¼ inches. Collection of the Brandywine River Museum, Gift of Betsy James Wyeth. © 1998 James Wyeth.

Tactile describes texture you know from your sense of touch. How would it feel to touch the subjects in **B** and **D**?

You know about other textures from your sense of sight. What textures do you see in **C**, **D** and **E**?

 E Vivi, Liestman Elementary. *Pig Mama*. Colored glue, crayon, oil pastels on paper, 18 by 12 inches.

Thinking Like an Artist 11

Community Keepsakes

Every community has artworks that have special meaning. Many of them are kept in **museums,** where they receive good care. Read the **credit lines** under **A**, **B**, and **C** to discover where each artwork is kept. What else can you learn from the credit line?

Look at the pictures on these pages. Why do you suppose these artworks hold special meaning in their communities?

What type of balance do you see in **A** and **B**? The jewelry in **C** shows **radial balance.** Its lines and shapes go out from the center. Point to the center of **C**.

A Artist unknown. Sioux. *Moccasins,* ca. 1890–1910. Leather, quills, glass beads, cotton thread, and sinew. Study Collection of the Plains Art Museum, Fargo, North Dakota.

B

Artist unknown.
Bentwood chest with lid, Haida, date unknown. Cedar, carved and painted with bear design, 12 by 16 by 10 inches. Department of Anthropology, Smithsonian Institution, Washington, D. C., catalog no. 74755.

C Artist unknown. *The Fuller Brooch*, English, 9th century. Silver and niello, diameter 4⅛ inches. The Trustees of The British Museum, London. © The British Museum, London.

D Angel, Zavala Elementary. *Wheelie the Shoe*. Marker, crayon on paper, 12 by 9 inches.

E Braulio, Zavala Elementary. *Dinoshoe*. Crayon, marker on paper, 12 by 9 inches.

How would you describe the textures in **A**, **B**, and **C**? Point to curved and straight lines. What other types of lines do you see? Which keepsake would you like to view in a museum? Tell why.

 Try Your Hand
Drawing a Shoe

Look at A.
Use a pencil to draw the outline of your shoe. Make it fill the paper.
Study your shoe closely and draw the details.
Is your shoe symmetrical? What is the texture of your shoe?
Now use your imagination to improve your shoe. Secret pockets, mirrors, springs, wheels—these are only a few ideas.
On another sheet of paper, draw your new and improved shoe.
Where will you display your drawings?

Thinking Like an Artist **13**

Georges Seurat

(zhorz soo-RAH)

(1859–1891)

Georges Seurat. *The Artist in His Studio,* ca. 1884. Conte crayon, 12⅛ by 9 inches. Philadelphia Museum of Art, A. E. Gallatin Collection.

What is the most important part of a painting? Georges Seurat thought that it was color. Seurat was born in Paris, France. He studied art during his school years. He spent long days in museums, where he learned about many of the great paintings. Later, Seurat made his own drawings. Most of these were in black and white.

Then Seurat began to study light and color. Soon he found a new way to paint. Instead of using lines, he used small dots of color. With this new way to paint, Seurat showed life in a city. He painted pictures of people at the circus. He showed people having fun outdoors.

Seurat spent as long as two years on a painting. First, he made many drawings of what he wanted to paint. Then, dot by dot, he carefully placed colors on the large canvas.

Seurat died at the age of 31. He finished only a few paintings in his short lifetime.

WRITE ABOUT ART

Look at *A Sunday on La Grande Jatte–1884*. What are the people doing?

Think of some ways to have fun at a park. Make a list. Write five things to do in a park. Use the painting to help you think of ideas.

When you make your list, remember to

- number your paper from 1 to 5.

- write only one idea next to each number.

- leave room at the bottom to tell about your favorite idea.

A Word About
A Sunday on La Grande Jatte–1884

This painting shows people enjoying a sunny afternoon in the park. The artist used tiny dots of color to show changes in light. How does he show the shady areas?
Would you like to visit this park? What games could you play there?

Write Away

Read your list of things to do in a park. Circle your favorite idea. Write about this idea. Tell why it is your favorite.

TALK ABOUT ART

 Georges Seurat. *A Sunday on La Grande Jatte – 1884*, 1884–1886. Oil on canvas, 83 by 123¼ inches. Helen Birch Bartlett Memorial Collection, 1926.224. Photograph © 1996, The Art Institute of Chicago. All rights reserved.

Look at A to answer these questions:

1. What do you see? The artist painted thousands of tiny dots for lines and shapes. Point to some tiny dots. If you stepped into this picture, would you feel you could move? What would you hear? Which textures might you touch or see? Do you see a group of people who remind you of your family? Explain.

2. How is the painting arranged? Which direction are most people facing? How did the artist show a center of interest? Why might the artist show the animals in motion?

3. What does the painting mean? Do the people in the painting look calm or nervous? What was the artist trying to say?

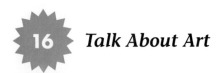

4. What's your opinion? Imagine that **A** is on a greeting card that you're writing to a friend. What might you say about the painting? Should your friend save the greeting card? Why or why not?

Compare A and B.

Read the titles of **A** and **B**. What is the subject of each painting? How are **A** and **B** alike? How are they different? Compare the center of interest in each painting.

 B Paul Klee. *Park near Lu(cerne)*, 1938. Oil and color paste on paper, mounted on jute burlap, 40 by 28 inches. Courtesy of Kunstmuseum, Bern, Switzerland and the Paul Klee Foundation, 1938.129. Photograph © AKG London.

A Word About

Park near Lu(cerne)

Paul Klee *(clay)* created a dreamlike design by using simple lines and shapes together. This imaginative painting shows that he liked artworks by children. Can you find trees in a park and children playing? What else do you see?

Unit 1 17

PORTFOLIO PROJECT

Drawing a Community Park
Will your drawing look like your favorite park?

1. Draw lines and shapes for people, animals, and trees in a park.
   Will you show a playground, too?

2. Color in your shapes.

3. Touch a tempera cake with your damp fingertip.
   Make dots to show some of the grass.

4. Wash your finger and touch another color.
   Fill in the grass with dots.

Will you make a sky with more dots? What else?
Do you like painting with your fingers? Explain.
Did you show motion in your drawing?

PORTFOLIO GALLERY

A

Stephanie, Zavala Elementary. *The Special Park.* Tempera cakes, marker on paper, 17 by 11 inches.

B

Janet, Zavala Elementary. *Walking My Dog in the Park.* Tempera cakes, marker on paper, 12 by 9 inches.

What Have You Learned?

Sketchbook Progress

1. Pick your favorite subject from your sketchbook. Why is this subject your favorite?

2. On another page of your sketchbook, draw your favorite subject again. This time add more details.

3. Use your Detail Detector to look closely at your finished drawing. Will you add more details?

4. How is your new drawing like your sketch? How is it different?

5. How are sketchbooks helpful to artists?

Portfolio Progress

Try Your Hand

6. What kinds of lines and shapes did you use in your drawing of a community event? Describe the details you included.

7. Did you draw a center of interest on each page in your flipbook? As you flip the pages, how do your drawings appear to be moving?

8. What type of balance did you use in your drawing of a shoe? How is your second drawing different from the first one?

Portfolio Project

9. Describe the colors in your drawing. Why did you choose these colors? Describe the shapes and types of lines you see.

10. Tell why you arranged the objects, people, and animals as you did. What decisions did you make as you planned this arrangement?

11. What meaning is expressed in your artwork?

12. List three things you think are successful about your artwork.

Unit Review

Teresa, A. J. Martin Elementary.
Symmetrical View. Construction
paper, 12 by 12 inches.

1. List the seven elements of art. Circle the names of the elements of art that you see in the artwork above.

2. List the seven principles of design. Circle the names of the principles of design that you see in the artwork above.

3. What is the center of interest of this artwork? How did the artist make this part the center of interest?

4. What is a detail?

5. Tell about two kinds of balance.

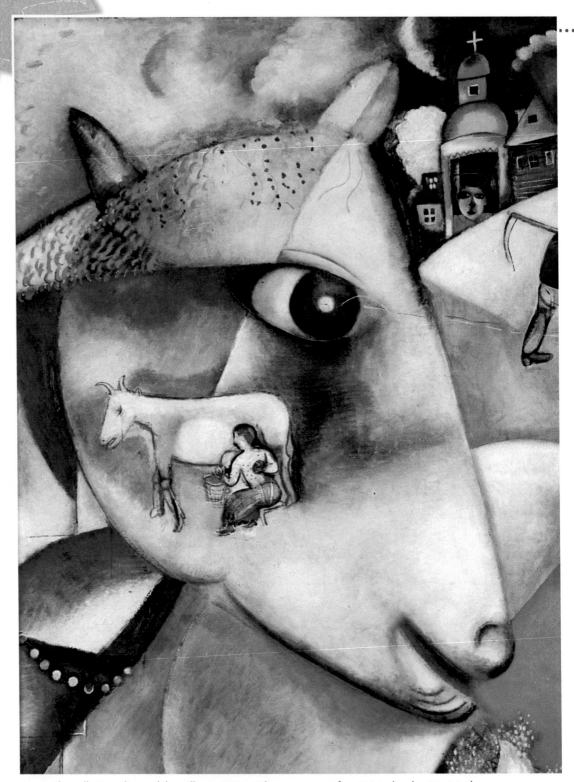

Marc Chagall. (Detail) *I and the Village*, 1911. Oil on canvas, 6 feet 3⅝ inches by 59⅝ inches. The Museum of Modern Art, New York, Mrs. Simon R. Guggenheim Fund. Photograph © 1996, The Museum of Modern Art, New York. © 1998 Artists Rights Society (ARS), New York/ADAGP, Paris.

Looking at Art

Artists have their own special ways of looking at the world. They see with imagination and a sense of wonder. Artists can discover a design in a puddle of water. They can find beauty in what others throw away. A trip through a junkyard can become an artist's treasure hunt.

This unit helps you find ideas for art in everyday places and in your dreams. It shows you how community pathways and vases of flowers can make you think about art.

Look for elements of art and principles of design around you. Let your imagination go. Be open to feeling a sense of wonder. You just might find yourself looking at art.

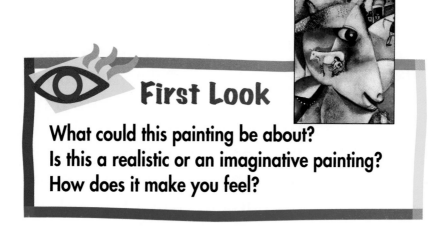

First Look

What could this painting be about?
Is this a realistic or an imaginative painting?
How does it make you feel?

Looking at Colors

Warm Colors

Cool Colors

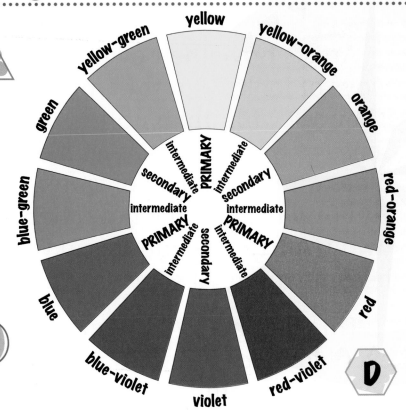

A

B

D

yellow-green · yellow · yellow-orange · green · orange · blue-green · red-orange · blue · red · blue-violet · violet · red-violet

PRIMARY · intermediate · secondary · intermediate · PRIMARY · secondary · intermediate · intermediate · PRIMARY · secondary · intermediate

C

The child in **C** is looking at many **hues,** or colors. Artists think of hues as being the members of the color community. Which hues can you name on these pages?

Look at **D**, the **color wheel.** It shows the community of colors. It helps artists see which hues to use. You can find color groups on the color wheel. **Primary colors**—yellow, red, and blue—make up a group. Point to the three primary colors. The three **secondary colors** are in between primary colors. Point to orange, violet, and green. Now find and name the six **intermediate colors.**

Katie, Woodridge Elementary. *My Cat.* Construction paper, tempera on paper, 18 by 12 inches.

F
Daniel, Woodridge Elementary. *Sunset.* Oil pastels on paper, 18 by 12¼ inches.

Look at **A** and **B**. They show members of color families—**warm colors** and **cool colors.** Warm colors are yellow, orange, and red. Cool colors are violet, blue, and green.

Related colors are next to each other on the color wheel. Some related warm colors are orange, red-orange, and red. Which picture shows warm colors? Why are these colors called "warm"? Name the warm colors in **E** and **F**. Related cool colors are blue-violet, blue, and blue-green. Which cool colors can you find in **B**? Why are these colors called "cool"? Name the cool colors in **E** and **F**.

 André Derain. *The Turning Road, L'Estaque*, 1906. Oil on canvas, 51 by 76¾ inches.
The Museum of Fine Arts, Houston, The John A. and Audrey Jones Beck Collection.

Pathways in Communities

Have you ever wondered which road to take? Pathways through communities have forever caught the attention of poets, musicians, and visual artists. Perhaps the mystery of where these paths might lead attracts artists.

Many artists have their own special **style,** or way of creating. The artists of **A** and **B** used a style with bright and bold colors. Each artist planned a **color scheme** showing a **variety** of different warm and cool hues. Name some warm and cool colors in **A** and **B**. Find places where two colors **blend** together to make another hue.

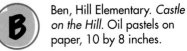 Ben, Hill Elementary. *Castle on the Hill*. Oil pastels on paper, 10 by 8 inches.

 David Hockney. *Mulholland Drive: The Road to the Studio*, 1980. Acrylic on canvas, 86 by 243 inches. Los Angeles County Museum of Art, purchased with funds provided by the F. Patrick Burnes Bequest. © David Hockney. Photograph © 1996, Museum Associates, Los Angeles County Museum of Art. All rights reserved.

The artworks on these pages are called **landscapes.** They show outdoor scenes. Point to shapes of hills, trees, fields, and pathways.

Notice how many of the shapes **overlap.** Some shapes are in front of others. This causes parts of some shapes to disappear.

In each artwork, the artist created a sense of space and **distance.** How do the sizes of the people in **A** help you see what is near and far away?

 Try Your Hand

Drawing a Landscape

Use your imagination to draw a landscape with oil pastels. Fill the whole page with bold and bright colors.

1. Choose three warm colors and three cool colors. You might blend some of them as you draw.
2. Begin drawing at the bottom of your paper to show shapes that are near.
3. Make some shapes overlap to show what's far away.

Will your landscape show a pathway?

Mixing Colors

PRIMARY
yellow

Intermediate
yellow-orange

Secondary
orange

Intermediate
red-orange

PRIMARY
red

Intermediate
red-violet

Secondary
violet

Intermediate
blue-violet

PRIMARY
blue

Intermediate
blue-green

Secondary
green

Intermediate
yellow-green

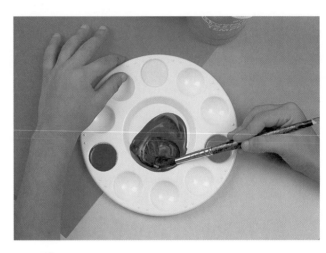

Mixing colors can be fun and magical. It's important to know how to do it. Otherwise you might end up with a muddy gray hue each time you try to mix colors.

A good way to learn is to practice. First, try mixing two primary colors to get a secondary color. Next, mix a primary color and a secondary color to get an intermediate color.

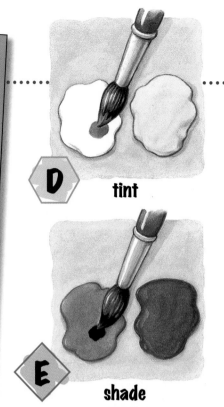

D tint

E shade

C

Micaela, Woodridge Elementary. *Portrait.*
Pencil, tempera on paper, 12 by 18 inches.

Finally, try mixing a dab of any color with white paint. Notice how the **value** of the color changes to a lighter **tint.** What happens when you mix a dot of black paint with a color? This darker value is called a **shade.**

Look at **C**. Point to primary, secondary, and intermediate colors. How did the artist make the tints and shades you see?

Seeing, Planning, Thinking Like an Artist

Explore ways to make different hues, tints, and shades by mixing paints. Use a large sheet of paper to practice mixing new colors. Put a few dabs of the new colors on a page in your sketchbook. Write some things you learned near each dab.

Mixing Colors 29

Gabriele Münter. *Blumen in der Nacht,* 1941. Oil on cardboard, 20 by 26 inches. Hamburger Kunsthalle, Hamburg. © 1996 Artists Rights Society (ARS), New York/VG Bild-Kunst, Bonn. Photograph by Elke Walford.

Flowers in Communities

In many communities you can find beautiful gardens. You might also see vases of flowers in windows or bowls of fruit on tables.

Artists like to paint pictures of flowers and fruits. They often arrange them in a **still-life** painting. A still life shows objects that don't move on their own, such as flowers, books, or food.

Notice the **space** in **A** and **C**. Most of it is used to show the flowers. Both paintings show flowers in an imaginative way. How do the artists' styles differ?

 Keith, Heflin Elementary. *A Bowl of Fruit.* Construction paper, oil pastels, 18 by 12 inches.

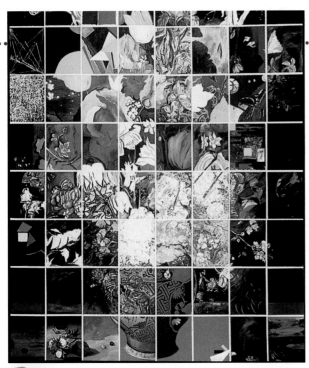

C Pat Steir. *The Brueghel Series (A Vanitas of Style)*, 1982–1984. Oil on canvas, 64 panels: each 28½ by 22½ inches. Courtesy Robert Miller Gallery, New York.

Look closely at **C**. The flowers in each rectangle are painted in a different style. The artist painted each rectangle to honor other artists whose works helped her learn. The rectangles help the parts of **C** fit together. They help give it **unity.** What helps us know that things in **A** go together?

D Christie, Justine, Pearl, Kelli, and Morgan, Hill Elementary. *Untitled.* Tempera on paper, 17⅞ by 23¾.

 Try Your Hand

Painting a Still-Life Puzzle

1. Look closely at a still life of flowers in a vase. Paint a picture and let it dry.
2. Make a puzzle. Fold your still life twice one way, then twice the other way. Open it and number each rectangle on the back side.
3. Cut out the rectangles as puzzle pieces.
4. Exchange some of them with your friends.
5. Glue together your puzzle, leaving small spaces in between.

How many different styles of flowers does your still life have ?

Looking at Portrait Prints

Elizabeth Catlett. *Sharecropper*, 1970.
Linoleum cut on paper, 18 by 17 inches.
National Museum of American Art,
Washington, D. C. © 1998 Elizabeth
Catlett/Licensed by VAGA, New York.

A **portrait** shows the likeness of a person or an animal—sometimes in a group. It can show only the face or include the body. Artists create portraits from memory, observation, and imagination.

The portraits on these pages are **relief prints.** They were made with **printing blocks.** Each artist created an image on the surface of a printing block.

Look at **A**. Point to different textures on the print. The artist used a sharp tool to carve lines and shapes in a linoleum printing block. She rolled printer's ink over the block and then gently pressed, then rubbed a paper over the inked block. Imagine her surprise when she pulled her print!

How to
Make a Monoprint

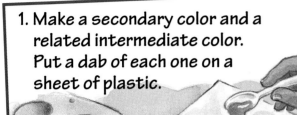
1. Make a secondary color and a related intermediate color. Put a dab of each one on a sheet of plastic.

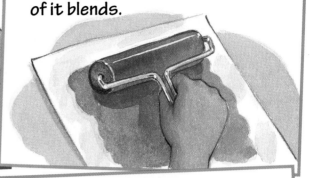
2. Roll the paint until only some of it blends.

3. Draw a picture in the paint with your finger, a pencil eraser, or a cotton swab.

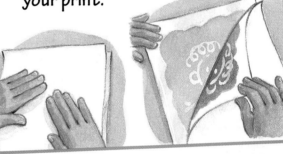
4. Gently press, then rub a paper over the printing block. Then pull your print.

After that, the artist improved the block by carving more details until she pulled the print she liked best. How many prints do you think she could pull from her final block?

Students made **monoprint** portraits in **B** and **C**. *Mono-* means "one." The design on the block survived only one print.

B Allie, Hill Elementary. *My Friend*. Tempera on construction paper, 9 by 12 inches.

 Try Your Hand
Making a Monoprint Portrait

Make a monoprint portrait of a friend. Use your memory, observation, or imagination to help you.

C Michael, Hill Elementary. *This is You*. Tempera on construction paper, 9 by 12 inches.

Kenojuak Ashevak. *Young Owl Takes a Ride,* 1984. Stonecut and stencil, 19½ by 25½ inches. © West Baffin Eskimo Co-operative Ltd.

Animals in Communities

Have you ever taken a piggyback ride? Look at **A** and its title. What is happening in the print? This artist created a portrait of animals from her community.

Point to different textures in **A**. Talk about the many types of lines and shapes. This relief print shows a variety of these art elements.

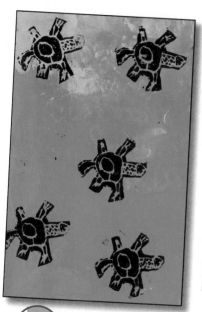

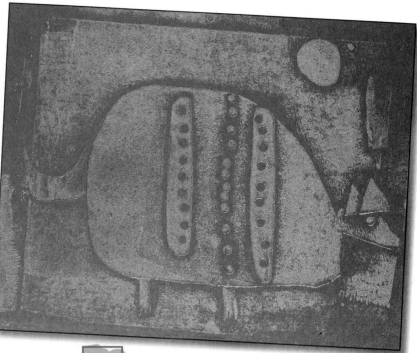

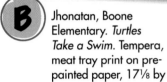
B Jhonatan, Boone Elementary. *Turtles Take a Swim*. Tempera, meat tray print on pre-painted paper, 17⅛ by 11⅛ inches.

C Katy, A. J. Martin Elementary. *Armadillo in Desert*. Printing ink on construction paper, 12 by 9 inches.

Artists can change their printing blocks in many ways. The artist of **A** carved into a flat stone. The artist of **B** glued thin shapes to her block. The artist of **C** drew a large shape in a meat tray. Which kind of print would you like to make? Why?

Try Your Hand
Making a Relief Print of an Animal

Create a relief print portrait of an animal. You can make a print in many ways.

To make a print like **B**, glue thin shapes to a cardboard block.

To make a print like **C**, draw an animal in a meat tray and cut it out.

Follow the steps on page 143 to finish your print.

Looking at Portrait Prints 35

Marc Chagall

(mark shuh-GAHL)

(1887–1985)

Marc Chagall. *Birthday (l'Anniversaire)*, 1915. Oil on canvas, 31¾ by 39¼ inches. The Museum of Modern Art, New York, acquired through the Lillie P. Bliss Bequest. Photograph © 1996 The Museum of Modern Art, New York. © 1998 Artists Rights Society (ARS), New York/ADAGP, Paris.

As a boy Marc Chagall loved to take walks in his Russian town. He walked past gray buildings covered in snow. He looked at small wooden houses and tall church steeples. Farther along, he saw people working in the fields and cows with big brown eyes. He felt that these things had a beauty all their own.

One day Chagall drew a portrait of a man. It was the first picture he had ever drawn. He began to draw more pictures. Soon, the walls of his room were covered with artwork. He had found a way to show others his view of the world.

Later, Chagall moved to a nearby city to learn more about art. He loved the city but was lonely there. He returned to his town often. On one visit he met the woman who later became his wife. It is thought that the painting above shows the artist and his wife. As Chagall expressed through his art, the couple was happy together. Theirs was a warm and loving family.

Next, Chagall moved with his wife to Paris, France. There he felt alive as never before. He went to art museums and talked with other artists. He became friends with poets. Paris became his home for much of his life.

WRITE ABOUT ART

A Word About
I and the Village

Look at *I and the Village*. Chagall created this painting from memory and imagination. It shows his ideas about the Russian village where he was born.

Do you see the artist? Many people think the green face is his. He chose colors based on his imagination. Why do you think he included animals in this painting?

Look at *I and the Village*. It shows animals, people, and houses. The artist may have seen these things as he took a walk in his town. Where do you take walks in your community?

Write Away

Think of a time you took a walk. What did you see? What did you hear? Write a story about the walk you took.

- First, tell where you took your walk.
- Next, tell what you saw and what you heard on your walk.
- Finish your story by telling how you felt at the end of your walk.

Marc Chagall. *I and the Village,* 1911. Oil on canvas, 6 feet 3⅝ inches by 59⅝ inches. The Museum of Modern Art, New York. Mrs. Simon R. Guggenheim Fund. Photograph © 1996 The Museum of Modern Art, New York. © 1998 Artists Rights Society (ARS), New York/ADAGP, Paris.

Look at A to answer these questions:

1. What do you see? What faces and figures can you see? Point to primary, secondary, and intermediate hues. Where do you see tints and shades? Which things appear upside-down?

2. How is *I and the Village* arranged? Tell about the variety of shapes you see. Point to things that overlap. Name some ways that the artist showed unity.

3. What does *I and the Village* mean? Why do you think Chagall used the circle to connect the calf and the person? What might this artist have been saying about his childhood?

4. What's your opinion? How does this painting make you feel? Would you choose it as a present for a friend? Why or why not?

 Rodolfo Morales. *Tarde de Nostalgia,* 1993. Oil on canvas, 59 by 40 inches. Private collection.

A Word About

Tarde de Nostalgia (Afternoon Memories)

To paint this colorful scene, Rodolfo Morales (ro-DAHL-fo mo-RA-lez) used his imagination and memory. It shows the village in Mexico where he grew up and returned to live about 12 years ago. "I came here to live in my memories," he said.

Which parts of the painting appear realistic? Which ones seem imaginative and about fantasy?

Compare A and B.

How did each artist show a dreamlike place? Discuss the groups of colors that are alike in **A** and **B**. Point to shapes that overlap in each painting. Which painting shows a crowded space? Which one shows an open space? How do these paintings make you feel?

PORTFOLIO PROJECT

Machine Gadget Prints

Does your community have a lot of machines? Use your imagination to discover how small, used gadgets can become printing tools.

1. Plan a design with warm and cool colors. It can be real or imaginary.

2. Dip gadgets into neon tempera paint and print them onto your paper.

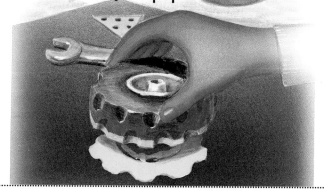

3. Overlap some of the shapes. Create a center of interest.

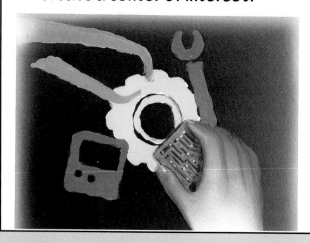

4. Let it dry. Then fill in spaces with a variety of chalk pastel lines and shapes.

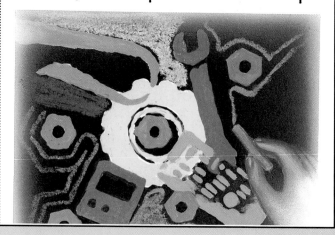

How did you blend your chalk pastel colors?
How might you look at machines differently now? Explain.
How else might gadgets help you make art?

PORTFOLIO GALLERY

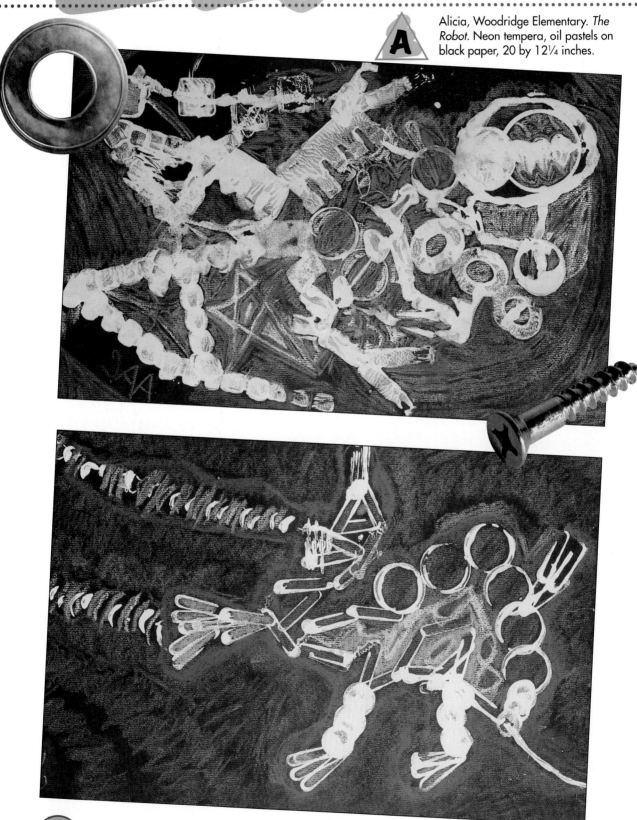

A Alicia, Woodridge Elementary. *The Robot*. Neon tempera, oil pastels on black paper, 20 by 12¼ inches.

 B Clayton, Woodridge Elementary. *The Dragon*. Neon tempera, oil pastels on black paper, 20 by 12¾ inches.

What Have You Learned?

Sketchbook Progress

1. What tints did you make in your sketchbook? Pick your favorite tint. Write the steps that you followed to mix it. Give this tint a name.

2. What shades did you make in your sketchbook? Pick your favorite shade. Write the steps that you followed to mix it. Give this shade a name.

Portfolio Progress

Try Your Hand

3. Name the warm and cool colors you used in your landscape. Did you overlap shapes? Which shapes appear close? Which ones seem farther away?

4. What hues and shapes did you use in your still-life puzzle? Do the pieces of your puzzle look good together? Why or why not?

5. Are the shapes in your monoprint portrait organic, geometric, or both? Explain.

6. Point out the center of interest in your relief print of an animal. What color scheme did you use for the background? How is a relief print different from a monoprint?

Portfolio Project

7. What gadgets did you choose for making your print? What are some reasons for your choices?

8. Did you use primary, secondary, or intermediate colors? Find the colors you used on the color wheel.

9. Does your print have unity? Explain.

10. Write a sentence that expresses your ideas about the meaning of your print. Then write three things you like about your print.

Unit Review

Lakela, Amelia Earhart Learning Center. *Exaggerated Colors in Nature.* Crayon, marker on paper, 12 by 18 inches.

1. Find at least eight places in the artwork on this page where shapes overlap. In your own words, explain what *overlap* means.

2. How would this artwork be different if no shapes overlapped? Explain.

3. Describe the most important part of this artwork. How did the artist make this the most important part?

4. The color groups that you learned about in this unit are primary colors, secondary colors, and intermediate colors. Make a list like the one below. Write the three hues that belong in each color group.

Primary Colors	Secondary Colors	Intermediate Colors
1.	1.	1.
2.	2.	2.
3.	3.	3.

5. What primary hues do you mix to make each secondary color?

6. What hues do you mix to make each intermediate color?

7. What hues are called warm colors? Why?

8. What hues are called cool colors? Why?

Looking at Art

Louise Nevelson. *Dawn's Wedding Chapel I*, 1959. Wood painted white, 90 by 51 by 6 inches. Courtesy of the Estate of Louise Nevelson. The Pace Gallery, New York. Photograph by Bill Jacobson.

Art Forms

Artists have different ways of expressing themselves. Some like to draw, print, paint, or make photographs. Others enjoy creating **sculpture.**

Sculpture is a type of **form.** Like other forms, sculpture takes up space. You can view some sculptures from more than one side.

This unit is about form. It shows you different types of sculpture in many places. What types of forms are in your community? Are some of them sculptures? Tell about those.

First Look

What are your thoughts about this sculpture?

Have you seen any of its parts in other places? Explain.

How does this artwork make you feel?

Forms in Your World

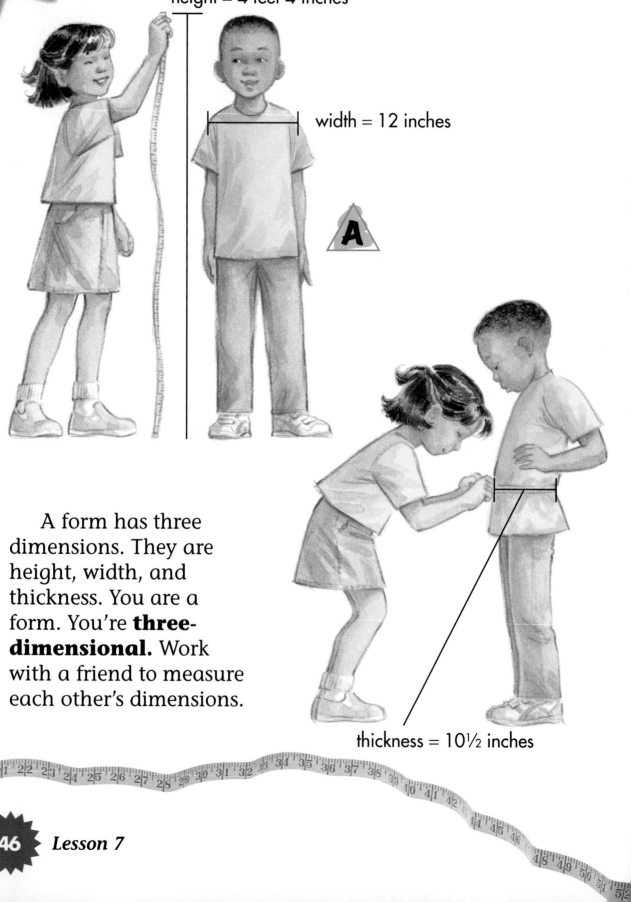

height = 4 feet 4 inches

width = 12 inches

A

thickness = 10½ inches

A form has three dimensions. They are height, width, and thickness. You are a form. You're **three-dimensional.** Work with a friend to measure each other's dimensions.

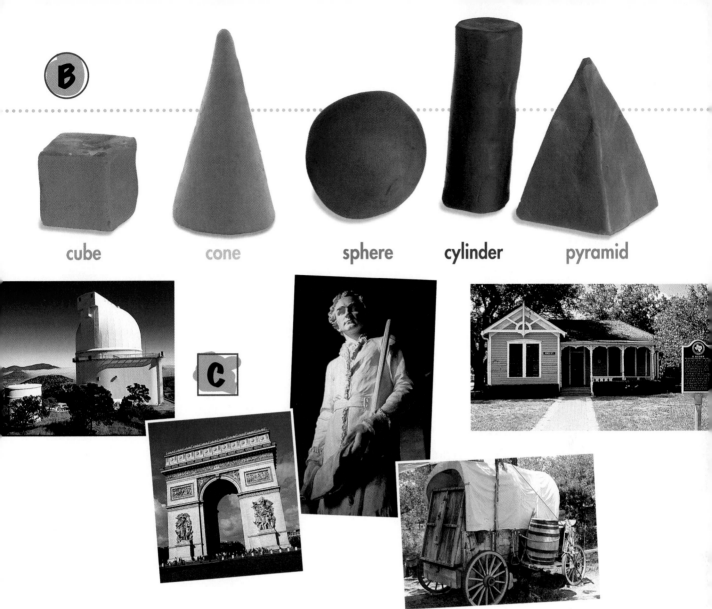

cube   cone   sphere   cylinder   pyramid

Name the different kinds of forms in **B**.
Point to some forms in **C** that match some forms in **B**.
Which other forms can you find around you?

Seeing, Planning, Thinking Like an Artist

Measure the dimensions of three different kinds of forms in
your classroom.
Make a sketch of each form and write down its dimensions.
Compare your forms with those of your friends.
How are the heights, widths, and thicknesses alike
and different?

Forms for Many Purposes

Artists make forms for many purposes. Sculptors made **A** and **B** for spiritual purposes. These sculptures are **symbols** of spiritual beliefs.

Each artwork is a part of a **tradition.** A tradition is something handed down from parents to children. Artists often use symbols to show what is most important in a tradition.

Some sculptures are made by **carving.** The sculptor cuts and takes away pieces from a solid material. The artist of **A** carved wood to make it. Carving is called a **subtractive** process.

Notice the position of each subject in these sculptures. Which one seems relaxed and is sitting still?

Artist unknown. *Guanyin (Bodhisattva of Compassion)*, China, dynasty Jin, 12th century, A.D. Carved wood, decorated in gold, lacquer, and polychrome, approximately 56½ by 35⅕ by 35⅕ inches. Hervey Edward Wetzel Fund. Courtesy Museum of Fine Arts, Boston.

 *Lesson 7*

The sculptor of **B** showed movement and imagination. The dancing subject moves with four arms.

You can see flickering flames from the sun around the subject. The flames are repeated to create **visual rhythm**.

 Artist unknown. *Nataraja: Siva as King of Dance.* South India, Chola Period, 11th century. Bronze, height 44½ inches. © The Cleveland Museum of Art, 1996, purchase from the J. H. Wade Fund, 1930.331.

 Try Your Hand
Creating Sculpture with Movement

1. Use toothpicks and small pieces of plastic foam.
2. Stick them together to show a person moving.
3. Use masking tape to hold things in place.
4. Cover your sculpture with aluminum foil.
5. Cover a foam base, too, and attach it to your sculpture.

C Elena, Cambridge Elementary. *Dancing Tin Man.* Toothpicks, foam, foil, 5 by 3¼ by 10 inches.

Forms in Your World 49

Sculpture Can Show Thoughts and Feelings

The subjects in **A** and **B** show **expression.** Their bodies and faces show thoughts or feelings. What do you suppose the subject of **A** is thinking? How might the subject of **B** feel?

You can find both **positive** and **negative space** in **A** and **B**. Most people see positive space first because it stands out from the background. Negative space is the background. It surrounds the positive space.

Notice how the sculptor used **proportion** in **B**. Compare the size of one part in relation to another. Do the hands appear large or small? Explain. What other parts have unusual proportions?

Auguste Rodin. *The Thinker*, 1880. Bronze, approximately 72 by 39⅕ by 58 inches. © Rodin Museum, Paris. Photograph © 1995 AKG London/Justus Göpel.

Artist unknown. *Smiling Figurine*, ca. 6th to 9th century A.D. Limestone, approximately 19¾ by 12¾ by 4½ inches. Museum of Anthropology at Xalapa, University of Veracruz, Mexico.

Look at the **patterns** of repeated lines and shapes in **B**. Some of these patterns are symbols for ideas and beliefs. The crisscross lines on the hat stand for movement. Now try to imagine the sculpture without patterns. How would the texture change?

Seeing, Planning, Thinking Like an Artist

Think about how your body looks and feels when you're happy, sad, or angry. Draw a picture of yourself in one or more of those moods.
How will your face show expression?

Sculpture Can Show Thoughts and Feelings **51**

Using Balance to Express Ideas

Artists sometimes use balance to express their ideas. The photograph of the sculpture in **A** shows **asymmetrical balance.** The parts are arranged differently on each side.

What feelings do you get from **A**? Why? How would you describe the proportions of this artwork? How does the title help you understand what the artist was trying to say?

How do **B** and **C** show asymmetrical balance? Each of these artists arranged an animal around a bowl. How might their sculptures be used?

 Genna, Woodridge Elementary. *Enchanted Horse.* Clay, colored glaze, clear glaze, 4¼ by 2½ by 5 inches.

 Mark, Woodridge Elementary. *Snake Effigy.* Clay, colored glaze, clear glaze, 5¼ by 4 by 1⅝ inches.

 Try Your Hand

Showing Asymmetry

Express yourself by creating a sculpture showing asymmetrical balance. Turn to page 145 and read about how to work with clay.

1. Use self-hardening clay to make a real or an imaginary animal.
2. Arrange the parts so that each side is different.
3. When your sculpture has dried, paint it.

Will your sculpture show patterns?

How will it make people feel?

How will you use it?

Sculpture Can Show Thoughts and Feelings

Art in Unusual Places

A sculpture's location often tells something about its meaning. Sometimes the place sets a **mood** for the sculpture. The mood, or feeling it gives you, might be serious or funny. Does anything seem unusual about the places the artists chose for **A** and **B**? Explain. What moods were the artists trying to show?

Sculptures are made of many types of materials. The artist of **A** made each back separately. She poured burlap mixed with glue into the same plastic mold. Each sculpture dried in a slightly different way. Point to differences in patterns of lines on the backs.

Magdalena Abakanowicz. *Backs*, 1976–80. Burlap and resin, each approximately 27 inches in height. © 1998 Magdalena Abakanowicz/Licensed by VAGA, New York/Marlborough Gallery, New York. Photograph courtesy Marlborough Gallery, New York.

A group of artists planned **B**. The artists thought of an unusual place for the cars. They arranged them in an unusual way. How would you feel about **B** if the cars were parked beside a curb in the city?

The direction of lines can add to the mood of an artwork. Some of the main lines in **A** go across in a **horizontal** direction. Others go up and down in a **vertical** direction. Horizontal and vertical lines often create a still, quiet mood. Point to horizontal and vertical lines in **A**.

The main lines in **B** are slanted. They go in a **diagonal** direction. Diagonal lines often create a busy, rowdy, unsteady mood. Point to diagonal lines in **B** and **C**.

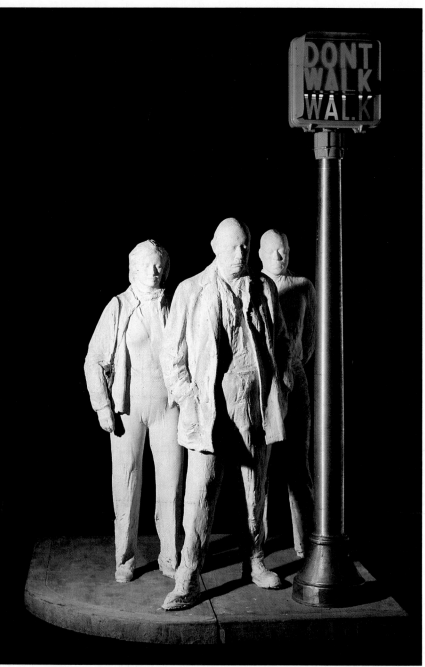

George Segal. *Walk, Don't Walk*, 1976. Plaster, cement, metal, painted wood, and electric light, 104 by 72 by 72 inches. Collection of Whitney Museum of American Art. Purchase, with funds from the Louis and Bessie Adler Foundation, Inc., Seymour M. Klein, President, the Gilman Foundation, Inc., the Howard and Jean Lipman Foundation, Inc., and the National Endowment for the Arts, 79.4. © 1998 George Segal/Licensed by VAGA, New York. Photograph © 1996, Whitney Museum of American Art.

Art Showing Ordinary Scenes

Some sculptors create artworks showing ordinary scenes. Many of these artworks are life-size and make you feel a part of them. They can be serious or funny, real or imaginary.

The artist of **A** created an **exterior,** or outdoor, scene. He made life-size plaster casts of people. He placed them in an ordinary place. What did he add to make the sculpture seem real? Why do you think the people are without expression? What did the artist do to make the people look alike? Does the scene look real or imaginary?

Red Grooms. *Subway* (detail from *Ruckus Manhattan*), 1976. Mixed media, 108 by 223 by 446 inches. © 1997 Red Grooms/Artists Rights Society. Photograph courtesy Marlborough Gallery, New York.

The artist of **B** created an **interior,** or indoor, scene. He used a variety of materials to make life-size forms of people riding in a life-size subway. A subway is an underground train that is an ordinary way of travel in many communities. Do the people in **B** look real or imaginary?

Try Your Hand
Creating an Interior Scene

Work in a small group to plan the interior of a school bus.

1. Cut off a long side of a shoe box to show the interior of the bus.
2. Decorate the interior with paper, glue, and markers.
3. Use modeling clay to form students and the driver.
4. Use other materials to add a variety of details.

Will the people look real or imaginary?

Patrick, Gunther, Wendy, Lucia and Stacy, Langford Elementary. *On the Way to School.* Shoe box, construction paper, markers, clay, 13 by 6½ by 5½ inches.

Art in Unusual Places 57

ARTIST AT WORK

Louise Nevelson

(lew-EEZ NEV-uhl-sun)

(1899–1988)

Louise Nevelson with her sculptures. Photograph © 1983 Jack Mitchell.

For Louise Nevelson, making art was almost like breathing. She was born in Russia. When she was six, her family moved to the United States. They settled in Maine. Her father sold lumber. The artist liked to make things out of her father's wood scraps. Early in life, she knew that she would be an artist.

Later, Nevelson studied art in Europe. Then she moved to New York. She began to see that art was all around her. She saw ideas for art even in things that others threw away. She started making sculptures from things she found. She used old boxes, table legs, and broken picture frames.

Nevelson glued or nailed her **found objects** together.

She arranged them in boxes. Then she assembled the boxes. She painted her **assemblages** black, white, or gold. Sometimes an assemblage filled the whole room.

Nevelson did not become well known right away. She worked for 30 years before people bought her artwork. But she did not give up. All her life, she believed in herself and in her art.

WRITE ABOUT ART

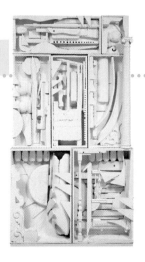

A Word About
Dawn's Wedding Chapel I

This wooden wall is made of boxes filled with found objects. Louise Nevelson gathered wooden forms that had been thrown away. She arranged them carefully inside the rectangles. Then she painted everything white to give her sculpture unity. Can you think of another reason?

Look at *Dawn's Wedding Chapel I*. The artist arranged pieces of wood in boxes to make her sculpture.

Suppose that you were about to make a wood sculpture like this one. How would you choose pieces of wood to use? How would you decide which pieces to put in each box? What would you use to hold the pieces in place?

Write Away

Write about the steps you would take to make your wood sculpture. Write the steps in order. Use time-order words: first, next, then, and last.

- Tell how you would choose wood pieces.
- Tell how you would decide which pieces to put in each box.
- Tell how you would hold the pieces in place.

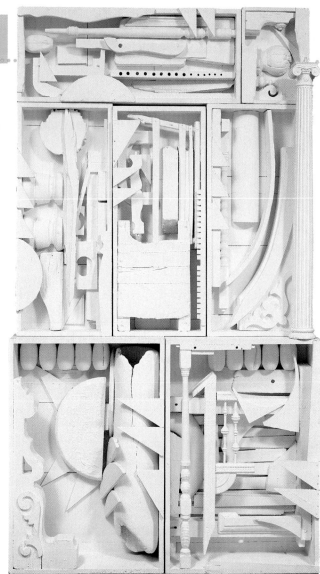

Louise Nevelson. *Dawn's Wedding Chapel I,* 1959. Wood painted white, 90 by 51 by 6 inches. Courtesy of the Estate of Louise Nevelson. The Pace Gallery, New York. Photograph by Bill Jacobson.

Look at A to answer these questions:

1. What do you see? Name some geometric forms in the assemblage. Point to horizontal and vertical lines. What other types of lines can you find? If you could touch the sculpture, how would it feel?

2. How is *Dawn's Wedding Chapel I* arranged? Point to a box that has a horizontal arrangement. Find objects that are overlapped. Find some examples of positive and negative spaces.

3. What does *Dawn's Wedding Chapel I* mean? What is the mood of this sculpture? How would the mood change if the artwork were painted many colors? Some say this wooden wall is like a poem with shapes and forms for words. Why?

4. What's your opinion? Would you exchange a wall in your home for this one? Tell why or why not. Have your feelings about this sculpture changed since you first saw it? Explain.

Compare A and B.

Which sculpture has many geometric forms? Which one has mostly organic forms? Compare the way each artist showed positive and negative spaces. Describe your mood when you look at A, then B.

Nancy Graves. *Tarot,* 1984. Bronze with poly-chrome patina and enamel, 88 by 49 by 20 inches. Courtesy of Knoedler & Company, New York. © 1998 Nancy Graves Foundation/ Licensed by VAGA, New York.

A Word About

Tarot

To make this sculpture, Nancy Graves gathered found objects. Through a special process, she made metal shapes and forms that looked like the found objects. Then she assembled and painted them. Can you name some of the objects used to create this sculpture?

PORTFOLIO PROJECT

Beauty in a Box

How can you make something beautiful of found objects? Try working with a friend.

1. Trim the edges from a cardboard box.

2. Plan several ways to arrange your found objects in the box.

3. Glue the objects in an arrangement that pleases you both. Let your assemblage dry.

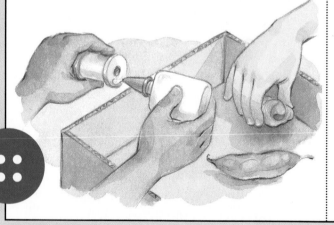

4. Add several drops of white glue to one color of tempera. Then paint your assemblage.

What do you like best about your found-object assemblage? What would you do differently next time? Think of a title with your friend.

A Elaine, Hill Elementary. *Untitled.* Cardboard box, found objects, glue, tempera, 12 by 6½ by 1¼ inches.

B Eric, Hill Elementary. *Untitled.* Cardboard box, found objects, glue, tempera, 12¾ by 6½ by 1¼ inches.

What Have You Learned?

Sketchbook Progress

1. Look at each page of your sketchbook. Make a list of each shape and form that you drew.

2. What forms did you measure in your classroom?

   • Which form was tallest? Which was shortest?

   • Which form was thickest? Which was thinnest?

   • Which form was widest? Which was narrowest?

3. In your sketchbook you drew a picture of yourself expressing a feeling. What expression does your drawing show?

Portfolio Progress

Try Your Hand

4. What dimensions can you measure in your foil-covered sculpture? Describe how you arranged the parts to show movement.

5. Give your asymmetrical sculpture a name. Describe how you arranged the parts of the sculpture to show asymmetrical balance.

6. As a group, list the important things you planned for the interior of your school bus. Have one member read the list for the class, while another points out each item on the model.

Portfolio Project

7. Is your box arranged symmetrically or asymmetrically? Explain.

8. Discuss with your partner the visual rhythm created in your assemblage. Find repeated lines, shapes, or forms that show rhythm.

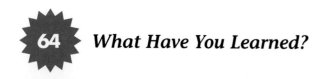

Unit Review

Katy, Cedar Creek Elementary.
Tuxedo Man. Clay, glaze, 1¼ by
1¾ by 3 inches.

1. What is the subject of the sculpture above?

2. Discuss the texture of this sculpture.

3. How did the artist use proportion?

4. How does this sculpture make you feel?

5. How would you define sculpture?

6. Are all forms sculpture? Explain your answer.

7. Explain how an artist makes a sculpture by carving.

8. Explain how an artist makes a sculpture by assembling objects.

Art Forms

Sofonisba Anguissola. (Detail) *The Chess Game*, 1555. Oil on canvas, 28¾ by 38¾ inches.
Museum Narodowe W. Poznaniu, Poznan, Poland.

Art Old and New

People, places, and animals are popular subjects in today's artworks. In fact, artists have chosen these subjects for thousands of years.

In this unit you will see old and new ways of showing people, places, and animals. Some of the artworks show ways that ideas, beliefs, and values have changed across the years. Others show ways they have stayed the same.

What about your own artworks? What subjects do they show? Has your style changed from last year? What else about your artwork might have changed? Has anything about it stayed the same? Explain.

 **First Look**

How can you tell that this is a close-up view of a painting?
What do you think the girls are doing?
Do you suppose the painting is from long ago,
    or is it modern? Explain.

Subjects Then and Now

Artist unknown. *The Flying Horse.* Eastern Han
dynasty, 2nd century A.D. Bronze, 13½ by
17¾ inches. Photograph © Robert Harding
Picture Library.

The sculpture in **A** was created almost 2,000
years ago in China. Why do you suppose this
sculpture is called *Flying Horse*? Does it look heavy
or light? What makes you think so?

Now look at the horse in **B**. It was painted in
Mexico about 50 years ago. Compared to **A**, it's a
modern artwork.

Describe the animals in **B**. Notice how the horse
overlaps the lion. How did the artist show that the
lion is fierce?

Rufino Tamayo. *Lion and Horse,* 1942. Oil on canvas, 36 by 46 inches. Washington University Gallery of Art, St. Louis, University Purchase, Kende Sale Fund, 1946. Reproduction authorized by the Foundation Olga and Rufino Tamayo, A.C.

The artist of **B** showed **contrast,** or a difference between light and dark colors. He placed tints next to shades—light colors next to dark ones. Notice how contrast helps you see the shapes better.

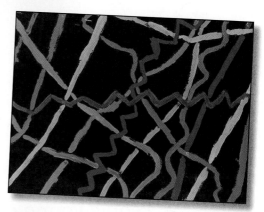

Marisol, Brooke Elementary. *Over and Under Lines.* Tempera on paper, 18 by 12 inches.

Seeing, Planning, Thinking Like an Artist

Practice painting overlapping lines.
1. On a large sheet of dark paper, paint a horizontal line with a light color. It can zigzag and bend.
2. Use another brush to paint a vertical line with a different tint. Make it stop and hop over the horizontal line.
3. Fill your paper with overlapping lines of different tints.
Stand back to view your painting. Why do the light colors show so well?

 Hung Liu. *Feeding the Rabbit,* 1995. Oil on canvas, 76 by 96 inches. Courtesy Steinbaum Krauss Gallery, New York. Photograph by Adam Reich.

Caring for Others Yesterday and Today

People young and old enjoy caring for others. Artists have expressed this in many ways. How did the artists of **A** and **B** show this?

Point to the center of interest in **A**. Notice how the children are looking and reaching toward the rabbit to show emphasis. How else did the artist of **A** show emphasis?

Notice the faces and bodies in **A** and **B**. Each subject in the paintings is shown in a natural **pose.** Instead of sitting still to face the viewer, the people are doing an activity. Each person holds a **prop** for the activity. Which props do you see in the paintings?

Lois Mailou Jones. *Mére du Senegal,* 1985. Acrylic on canvas, 24 by 36 inches. From the collection of the artist.

Luis, Allison Elementary. *All My Friends.* Oil pastels on paper, 18 by 12 inches.

Point to geometric and organic shapes in **A** and **B**. Find patterns of colors and shapes. Where did each artist show shapes that overlap? Explain how tints and shades in each painting create contrast.

 Try Your Hand
Drawing Your Friends

Make a drawing of a group of friends in a natural pose.
What prop will they use to help create a center of interest?
1. Use a large sheet of paper and oil pastels.
2. Draw your friends from memory or imagination.

Subjects Then and Now

Faces Then and Now

Red Grooms. *Dali Salad*, 1980–1981. Color lithograph and silkscreen cut out, glued, and mounted on rag paper (edition of 55), 26½ by 27½ by 12 inches. Courtesy Brooke Alexander Gallery, Inc., New York. Photograph © D. James Dee, New York.

Giuseppe Arcimboldo. *Summer,* 1563. Oil on limewood, 30½ by 20 inches. Kunsthistorisches Museum, Vienna, Austria. Photograph © Erich Lessing/Art Resource, New York.

Portraits of faces can be funny or serious. They can be likenesses of real or imaginary people. How would you describe the people on these pages?

The artist used his imagination to show the person in **A**. Why do you think the painting is called *Summer*? The subject of **B** was a well-known modern artist named Salvador Dali (SAL-vuh-door DAH-lee). Why do you suppose the portrait is called *Dali Salad*?

Notice the expressions in **A** and **B**. Which feelings do they show? Which portrait shows a side view, or **profile**? Which one shows a front view, or **frontal** pose?

C Kristin, Woodridge Elementary. *Self-portrait.* Tempera on paper, 11⅜ by 14 inches.

D Adriana, Brooke Elementary. *Curly Rock.* Rock, tempera, pipe cleaners, construction paper, 4½ by 8 by 4½ inches.

Artists often follow guidelines when they create a portrait. For example, they usually show the eyes about halfway between the top of the head and the bottom of the chin. A student painted her own portrait, or **self-portrait**, in **C**. Do you think she planned where to place the eyes?

Try Your Hand
Painting a Rock

Paint a face on a rock.
1. Use your imagination to find a face on your rock.
2. Use paint and markers to show the face.
3. Paint the facial features.
4. Add details with cut paper, glue, pipe cleaners, and other objects.

Will your portrait be a profile or a frontal pose?
What expression will you show?

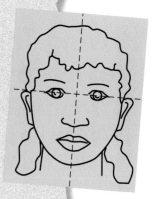

Artist unknown. *Stela of the steward Montuwosre,* Egyptian, dynasty 12 (ca. 1955 B.C.). Painted limestone, 41 by 19⅝ inches. The Metropolitan Museum of Art, Gift of Edward S. Harkness, 1912. (12.184). © 1983 The Metropolitan Museum of Art.

A is about 3,000 years old. It shows Egyptian children thanking their father. Their grandfather stands above them. What gifts do you see? Why do you suppose the children were thankful?

Artists of different cultures often create in a **cultural style.** This style shows something about when, where, and how they live. Look closely at **A** to discover something about the cultural style of this ancient Egyptian artist. Notice how each person is shown in both a profile and a frontal view.

Giving Thanks Yesterday and Today

A **culture** is a group of people who share ideas, beliefs, and values. Each culture has its own way of doing things. The portrait in

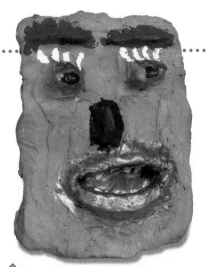

Juan, Brooke Elementary. *Untitled.* Clay, acrylic paint, 3½ by 6 by 2¼ inches.

Joe, Brooke Elementary. *Untitled.* Clay, acrylic paint, 4½ by 5½ by 1½ inches.

The story above the people is written in symbols. Try to guess what a few of the symbols in **C** might mean. Why do you suppose the artist made the sizes of the people so different?

The portrait in **A** is called a **relief sculpture.** Parts of a stone were carved away to make other parts stand out from the background. Point to parts that stand out. This sculpture was made using a subtractive process.

 Try Your Hand

Making a Clay Sculpture

Make a relief sculpture with clay. Look on page 145 to help you.
1. Carve a self-portrait to show how you feel when you give a present to someone special.
2. Let it dry.
3. Paint the parts that stand out.
Will you show a profile or a frontal pose—or both? Will you include any symbols?

Architecture Then and Now

Artist unknown, Mayan. *El Castillo/Pyramid of Kukulcan,* 11th–13th century. Chichén-Itzá, Yucatán, Mexico.

People have always needed shelter from the weather. What are some other kinds of buildings that people need?

Artists who plan buildings are called **architects.** They create plans for **architecture,** a three-dimensional type of art. Name some forms in the buildings shown in **A** and **B.**

The structure in **A** is a type of pyramid. This temple in Mexico was designed by Mayan architects more than 1,000 years ago. Does the temple look heavy or light? Explain.

R. Buckminster Fuller, architect. *Geodesic Dome*. American Pavilion, Expo '67, 1967, Montreal, Canada.

 Lisa, Eanes Elementary. *House for a Giraffe*. Crayon, marker on paper, 17 by 11 inches.

The structure in **B** is a modern dome in Canada. This lightweight building saves energy and was built with low-cost parts. The architect planned the design to solve many problems in the world. How might it be used underwater? What other problems might it solve?

Seeing, Planning, Thinking Like an Artist

Create a plan for an animal house.
1. Conduct an imaginary interview with an animal. Find out all its housing needs. Make a list.
2. On a large sheet of paper, draw a plan for the house. Make the front wall invisible. Show what is inside.

Architecture Then and Now

 The Louvre, Paris, France

Old and New Together

The buildings in **A** and **B** are parts of an art museum in Paris. It is one of the largest art museums in the world. You can see paintings, sculptures, and other artworks inside. About 800 years ago, the museum was a fortress. Later it was a palace for kings and queens. About 200 years ago, it became an art museum.

Picture **A** shows a street side of the museum. To find the entrance, you can go through the round **arches.** Round arches were invented by architects in Rome about 2,000 years ago. Point to the round arches in **A**.

I.M. Pei, architect. Entrance to the Louvre, Paris, France.

The arches lead to a courtyard where you can see a big surprise. The entrance to the museum is a modern glass pyramid! Pools of water reflect its form. Look at **B** to see the old and new architecture together. You can enter the pyramid and ride down an escalator. It takes you to a large open space beneath the pyramid. To begin your tour, you could choose any of the underground spaces, which lead to artworks in the older buildings.

Try Your Hand
Designing a New Entrance
Plan a new entrance to your school.
Think about where it should be and how it will be used.
Draw from imagination. Show the school building, too.

ARTIST AT WORK

Sofonisba Anguissola

(so-fo-NEES-buh ahn-gwee-SO-lah)

(1532–1625)

Sofonisba Anguissola. *Self-portrait,* 1554. Wood, 6¾ by 4¾ inches. Kunsthistorisches Museum, Vienna, Austria. Photograph by Erich Lessing/Art Resource, New York.

Sofonisba Anguissola lived in Italy long ago. At that time most people felt that girls should learn to sew and to play music. They believed only boys should study school subjects. Some boys studied art with a master teacher for many years. They learned to draw and paint.

Anguissola's parents wanted their six daughters to study many things. When the artist was about 14 years old, her father saw that she could draw well. He sent her to study art. After she had studied for several years, people began to ask her to paint pictures of their family members.

One day the king of Spain heard about Anguissola. He asked her to become a painter in his court. She made the long journey from Italy to Spain. She lived in the queen's household while she painted portraits of children, women, and men. These paintings are a record of history. They show how people lived at that time.

WRITE ABOUT ART

A Word About
The Chess Game

This portrait shows three of the six girls in the artist's family long ago. They are playing a table game. No one knows whether one of the girls is the artist herself. Nor do they know who is the older woman watching the game. A popular art critic at that time wrote about the painting, ". . . It was done with such [skill] that they all seemed truly alive and only lacking in speech."

Look at *The Chess Game*. It shows two sisters playing chess while another sister and a woman watch. What games do you play with your sisters, brothers, or friends? Do you play hide-and-seek or tag? Perhaps you play board games like the girls in the painting.

Write Away

Think of a time that you enjoyed playing a game. Write a free-verse poem about it. A free-verse poem sounds like a person talking. Here is an example.

Summer Tag

It's a warm summer evening.
I'm playing tag with my friends.
I'm It.
Latasha runs toward the bushes.
Tomás dashes into the shadows.
I run after Latasha and touch her shoulder.
We shout. We laugh.
Lightning bugs flash.
Now I run away from Latasha.
I run faster than the flash of a lightning bug.

TALK ABOUT ART

Sofonisba Anguissola. *The Chess Game*, 1555. Oil on canvas, 28¾ by 38¾ inches. Museum Narodowe W. Poznaniu, Poznan, Poland.

Look at **A** to answer these questions:

1. What do you see? Why might you say that these people are in a natural pose? Who seems aware of the artist? Explain. Point to a frontal view, and then to a profile. What did the painter use as a main prop?

2. How is the painting arranged? Point to places where the artist showed contrast. How did she use patterns to show unity?

3. What does the painting mean? What role might the woman on the right play in the girls' lives? What was the artist saying about her sisters?

4. What's your opinion? Would you like to join the game shown in the painting? Explain. Have your feelings about this painting changed since you first saw it? Explain.

Henri Matisse. *Pianist and Checker Players*, 1924. Oil on canvas, 29 by 36⅜ inches. Collection of Mr. and Mrs. Paul Mellon, Photograph © 1996 Board of Trustees, National Gallery of Art, Washington, D. C. © 1998 Succession H. Matisse, Paris/Artists Rights Society (ARS), New York.

Compare A and B.

How are the colors and shapes alike? How are they different? What do the clothing styles tell you about each painting? How are the backgrounds different? What can you learn about the way these people lived by studying these paintings?

A Word About
Pianist and Checker Players

This painting shows an interior scene in France about 75 years ago. While children quietly play a table game, a woman plays the piano in the colorful, patterned room. Try to imagine the sounds and smells around them.

Unit 4 **83**

PORTFOLIO PROJECT

Planning a Treehouse

Can you imagine a game room in a tree?

1. Make sketches with friends. Have your game room include an entrance, a table and chairs, and ways to make it safe.

2. Place a small tree branch in a can. Hold it in place with rocks.

3. Build your game room with cardboard, craft sticks, string, a glue stick, paper, and scissors.

4. Make some people with colored wire or modeling clay. What else will you add to your game room?

How will your game room protect people from the rain?
What types of games would you like to play there?
Could the same game room have been designed long ago?
Explain.

A

Juan, Leslie, Mayra, Socorro, and Vanessa, Brooke Elementary. *Our Treehouse*. Tree branch, construction paper, wire, craft sticks, pipe cleaners, string, 19½ by 18½ by 28 inches.

B

Adriana, Connie, Jesus, Mireya, and Ramon, Brooke Elementary. *Our Game Room*. Tree branch craft sticks, string, construction paper, wire, pipe cleaner, 25 by 13¾ by 30 inches.

What Have You Learned?

Sketchbook Progress

1. Look in your sketchbook at the house you planned for an animal. Read the questions you wrote. How are they like the questions an architect must answer before planning a building?

Portfolio Progress

Try Your Hand

2. Discuss with a friend the positive and negative spaces in your group portrait. Do any shapes overlap? Point to areas where you used contrast to emphasize shapes.

3. Write a description of your painted rock so that someone who has never seen it could find it in your classroom.

4. What details did you carve into your relief sculpture to show your feelings? Did you include any symbols? If so, describe them. What is their special meaning to you?

5. What is special about the new entrance you planned for your school? How does your drawing show old and new together?

Portfolio Project

6. Close your eyes and think about being in your treehouse game room. Then write a paragraph about how it would feel to visit this place. What sounds might you hear? What would you see below? Describe other feelings you would have.

Unit Review

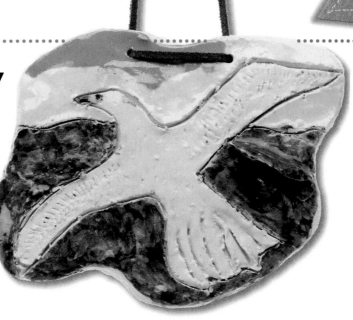

Tara, Maplewood Elementary. *Over the Waves.* Clay, glaze, 8¼ by 5¾ by 1 inches.

1. What is the subject of the artwork?

2. Explain how the colors show contrast.

3. Explain how overlapping helps you see what is near and what is far away.

4. Is the pose shown in this artwork a frontal view or a profile view?

5. Are the shapes geometric, organic, or both?

6. Describe how the artist used emphasis to make the center of interest.

7. Describe any textures you see in this artwork.

8. What is a portrait? What is a self-portrait?

9. What types of artworks do architects design?

10. Describe how you are seeing ideas for art in the world around you.

Beverly Buchanan. (Detail) *St. Simons*, 1989. Oil pastel on paper, 38 by 50 inches. © 1989 Beverly Buchanan. Courtesy Steinbaum Krauss Gallery, New York. Photograph by Gamma One Conversions, New York.

Many Ways to Express

Most people have special ways of expressing their thoughts and feelings. Acting, playing music, singing, and dancing are some fine art expressions. You've also learned about many ways that people express themselves through another one of the fine arts—the visual arts.

This unit describes yet more types of visual art expression. It shows ways that artists express thoughts and feelings with line, shape, and color. It explains how some artists express themselves through camera and computer arts.

How do you like to express yourself? Can you think of more than one way? Which type of visual art would you like to learn more about?

 First Look

What type of structure do you see?
What is unusual about the lines and colors of this structure?
How does it make you feel?

Expression Through Line, Shape, and Color

Julie, Petrosky Elementary.
I Quilt! Hand-stitched
painted fabric, wire
hanger with wooden
heart, 9 by 13 inches.

B

A

Faith Ringgold. *Harlem Renaissance Party:
Bitter Nest, Part II*, 1988. Acrylic on canvas,
printed, tie-dyed, and pieced fabric, 94 by
82 inches. © 1988 Faith Ringgold, Inc.

The pictures on these pages show some ways that artists use line, shape, and color. These and other elements of art are tools of expression.

Point to lines, shapes, and colors in **A**. You can read a special story along two borders of this **story quilt.** The story is about a group of artists who formed a community in New York City about 75 years ago. They shared new ideas and materials for creating art. Using her imagination, the quiltmaker painted some of those artists at a dinner party.

D Kathryn, Woodridge Elementary. *Untitled*. Black glue, oil pastels, tempera on paper, 11 by 15 inches.

C

Leonardo da Vinci. *Self-portrait*. Manuscript drawing, chalk on paper. Biblioteca Reale, Turin, Italy. Scala/Art Resource, New York.

The artist who drew the self-portrait in C lived 500 years ago in Italy. His community was especially interested in the arts, sciences, and new ideas. He filled many sketchbooks with plans for inventions. What do you notice about the lines in C, which were drawn with chalk? Did the artist show the edges of his own face? Explain.

Seeing, Planning, Thinking Like an Artist

Plan a party for a group of friends who share a common interest. Sketch a design for an invitation.

Expression Through Line, Shape, and Color 91

Expression as a Style

Wassily Kandinsky. *Grüngasse in Murnau*, 1909. Oil, gouache and watercolor on cardboard, 13⅕ by 17⅘ inches. Städtische Galerie im Lenbachhaus, Munich. Photograph © AKG London.

Some artists share a special style of art that sets their artworks apart from others. The paintings on these pages show the style of **German Expressionists.** This community of artists painted together in Germany almost 100 years ago. Today many German Expressionist paintings hang in the museum shown in **B.**

German Expressionists often set up their **easels** outdoors to paint exterior scenes. Their **palettes** were filled with bright, bold colors of paint. Which painting shows an exterior view?

Städtische Galerie im Lenbachhaus, Munich, Germany.

 Gabriele Münter. *Listening*, 1909. Oil on cardboard, 19⅞ by 26½ inches. Städtische Galerie im Lenbachhaus, Munich. © 1996 Artists Rights Society (ARS), New York/VG Bild-Kunst, Bonn.

Look closely at the **brush strokes** in both **A** and **C**. How would you describe the way these artists applied paints?

The subject of **C** was another artist in the community. How do you feel about the colors of this portrait?

Try Your Hand

Painting with Expression

Paint a picture in the style of German Expressionists.
Show an interior or an exterior scene.
Which colors will you choose?

Expression Through Line, Shape, and Color 93

Expression Through Camera Arts

Have you ever spilled a glass of milk? The **photographer** of **A** captured a splash of milk on **film.** A still photography **camera** can stop the action of such a moment in time.

Many of today's still photography cameras are easy to use. Just follow some basic steps to take a **photograph** with them.

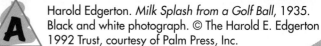
Harold Edgerton. *Milk Splash from a Golf Ball,* 1935. Black and white photograph. © The Harold E. Edgerton 1992 Trust, courtesy of Palm Press, Inc.

1. **Compose,** or plan, your photograph by looking through the viewfinder. Make sure the sun is behind you. Turn the camera to compose a vertical or horizontal picture.

2. With elbows at your sides, hold your camera steady.

3. Press a button to take the picture.

B

C Ulises, Brentwood Elementary. *The Nose Knows.* Black and white photo copy, colored markers, 8½ by 11 inches.

Photographs can be taken with color or black-and-white film. Color film shows interesting hues. Black-and-white film shows contrast between light and dark areas. **Shading** helps you see gradual changes between those areas. Point to shading in **A**.

The photocopies in **B** and **C** were taken by the camera inside a photocopy machine. A student artist arranged objects on the glass plate. The objects were almost flat. Next he carefully lowered the cover and pressed a button. Finally he colored his photocopy with **complementary** colors, or two colors opposite each other on the color wheel. How did the colored markers change the photocopy?

Seeing, Planning, Thinking Like an Artist

Which flat objects do you have for making a photocopy design?
Arrange them on your desk.
Make a sketch of your best arrangement.
Use markers to color your design in a complementary color scheme.

David Hockney. *Mother, Los Angeles, Dec. 1982*, 1982. Photographic collage, 53 by 39 inches. © David Hockney.

Photographs About People

Some photographers create photographs with people as subjects. The photographer of **A** created a **photomontage** of his mother. He took many photographs and then arranged them together. How does this photomontage add visual rhythm to still photography?

Many photographers compose photographs indoors in a **studio.** Others work outdoors in the natural environment. Where do you think the photographer shot **B**?

C

Travis, Brentwood Elementary. *Thinking*. Photocopy and photographic montage, 9 by 12 inches.

B

Shawn Nixon (age 18). *Boxcar Pose,* 1990. Photograph, silver print. 20 by 16 inches. Courtesy of Shooting Back, Inc.,Washington, D.C.

D

Lorranec, Brentwood Elementary. *On Vacation*. Photocopy and photographic montage, 9 by 12 inches.

Try Your Hand

Creating a Photomontage

1. Ask your teacher to help you photocopy your own drawing or photograph of someone special.
2. Make about six photocopies in the same or different sizes.
3. Color them with your favorite color scheme.
4. Arrange them on poster board. Add colored shapes and images cut from magazines.
5. Glue your best arrangement.

How do the magazine cutouts tell more about your subject?

Expression Through Computer Arts

A

The computer has become an important art tool. Like pencils, paintbrushes, and scissors, computers help artists express themselves. Artists can draw, paint, cut, paste and print using a computer. Artists can even use computers to make photographs.

The artist in **A** uses a computer to paint and draw images. Computer artists often work in office buildings and in their homes. Their tools can include a microcomputer with keyboard, color monitor, and mouse. Other tools include a color printer, a scanner, a modem, and software with art programs. Would you like a career as a computer artist?

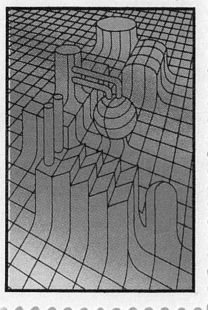

Science & Industry
USA 20c

B

Saul Bass. *Science & Industry*, 1983.
U.S. postage stamp, computer-aided
design. © United States Postal Service.

Computer artworks are used in many ways. The postage stamp in **B** was designed by a computer artist. He wanted to show how science and industry can work together. How do the lines, shapes, and colors help you understand ways that science and industry cooperate?

C Jardian, Brentwood Elementary. *The Fortress*. Computer-generated stamp design, 11 by 8½ inches.

Seeing, Planning, Thinking Like an Artist

Make some sketches of a postage stamp design. Use lines, shapes, and colors. What idea will your design show?

If you have a computer with software for drawing or painting, make your design on the screen. Save it in your digital sketchbook. Print it out and display it.

D Andre, Brentwood Elementary. *Rainbow Trout*. Computer-generated stamp design, 11 by 8½ inches.

Expression Through Computer Arts 99

More Art Technology

You've learned a lot about camera arts and computer arts. But these two **media** offer even more ways for artists to express themselves. You may want to experiment with the technology ideas on these pages.

The print in **A** was made on a computer. Look closely to see many layers of lines and shapes in the print. Point to places where they overlap. Like traditional printmakers, artists who make computer prints train themselves to work with layers. How is this computer print like prints you've made? How is it different?

Karen Guzak. *Jewels for Taj,* 1987. 13-plate color lithograph, with hand-drawn and computer-drawn images, 22 by 29 inches. Courtesy of the artist.

100 *Lesson 15*

 Nam June Paik and John Godfrey. *Global Groove*, 1973. Video. Produced by the Television Laboratory at WNET/13. Courtesy of Electronic Arts Intermix, New York.

The artist of **B** layered images with another type of **technology.** The medium he used was **videotape.** By joining parts of many videotapes and film together on a screen, he created a moving photomontage. Why do you suppose he called his artwork a "time collage"?

Beverly Buchanan

(BEV-uhr-lee byu-CAN-uhn)

(1941–   )

Beverly Buchanan

When Beverly Buchanan was a child, her family went to the beach. She spent more time looking at buildings than playing in the water. Years later, as an artist, she is still interested in buildings. The artist grew up in North Carolina. She worked in the field of health. At the same time, she studied art. After a few years, she chose to work as an artist full time. She lived for a while in New York. Then she moved to Georgia.

Buchanan has made many kinds of artworks. Some are large stone or cement sculptures. She made these to be placed outdoors. The sculptures blend in with the things around them.

When she traveled through the Georgia countryside near her home, Buchanan saw small, roughly made houses. She wanted to share the beauty she saw in these simple buildings. She began making sculptures in the form of these homes. She also made paintings and drawings of them. Through her art, Buchanan found a way to honor the people who called these buildings home.

WRITE ABOUT ART

Look at *St. Simons*. It shows how one kind of home looks from the outside.

A Word About

St. Simons

This colorful drawing shows the artist's feelings for her community. It is an expression of love for a culture she knows well. Which sounds, smells, and sights do you suppose might have come from within this home?

Write Away

Think about the home you live in or another one you have seen. What does it look like from the outside? Is it a home for one family or for many families? Does it have a porch? How many windows does it have? What color is it?

- Paint a word picture of this home.
- Write about how it looks from the outside. Be sure to tell about the front, sides, and back of the home.

My home is ten stories high.

My grandmother's house is white.

My friend's house is made of mud and straw.

TALK ABOUT ART

Beverly Buchanan. *St. Simons*, 1989. Oil pastel on paper, 38 by 50 inches. © 1989 Beverly Buchanan. Courtesy Steinbaum Krauss Gallery, New York. Photograph by Gamma One Conversions, New York.

Look at A to answer these questions:

1. What do you see? Describe the types of lines you see. Name some shapes you see. What do you notice about the doors on the houses? What do you think the colors behind the houses represent?

2. How is the drawing arranged? What is the center of interest? Explain. Discuss the visual rhythm in this drawing. Tell how the artist used both unity and variety in her drawing.

3. What does the drawing mean? Why do you think the artist used such bright colors? What parts of the drawing seem imaginary? What parts seem real? What was the artist saying about these homes?

4. What's your opinion? Would you draw your community with bold colors and busy lines? Tell why or why not. Have your feelings about this drawing changed since you first saw it? Explain.

Compare A and B.

Name some ways that **A** and **B** are alike. How are the artworks different? Why might the artists have made the doorways different sizes? What is special about each medium? Explain.

 B Ben Livingston. *Neon Mural #1*, 1987. Neon, computer-animated story, 14 by 40 feet. © Ben Livingston. Photograph © Carrington Weems.

A Word About
Neon Mural #1

This colorful scene by Ben Livingston is part of a neon cartoon. The lights are controlled by a computer. The artwork appears on the front of the artist's studio. The artist used neon lights to outline his door. Then he added an outline of a make-believe house, a flower, and a night sky. The artist even made a neon portrait of his cat. What kind of scene could you show with neon lights?

PORTFOLIO PROJECT

High-Tech Design

Which structure in your community is special to you? Is it a house, an apartment building, a store, or another structure? Why is it special?

1. Arrange flat objects to show the lines of your structure.

2. Glue your best arrangement to a 9-inch by 12-inch sheet of poster board. Let it dry.

3. Make a photocopy of your design.

4. Add color with markers or neon tempera paint.

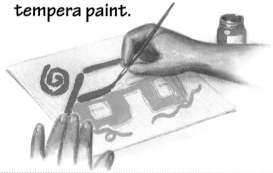

5. Glue your artwork to another sheet of poster board.

6. Display your artworks together!

How is your picture of a high-tech structure like the one in your community? How is it different? What is special about your artwork?

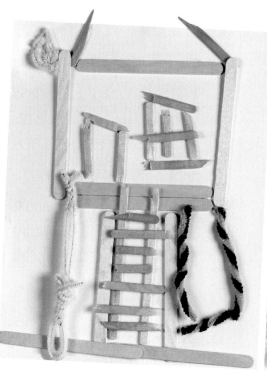

Andre, Brentwood Elementary. *Our Fun House*. Craft sticks, pipe cleaners, tempera on paper, 8½ by 11 inches.

Bethany, Brentwood Elementary. *On Top of the Capitol*. Craft sticks, pipe cleaners, tempera, 8½ by 11 inches.

What Have You Learned?

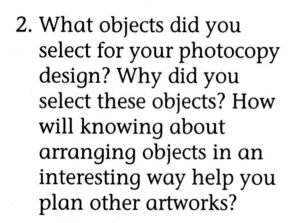

Sketchbook Progress

1. Would the invitation in your sketchbook make your friends want to come to your party? Give two reasons why. Use your sketchbook to design an invitation to a party where everyone has different interests.

2. What objects did you select for your photocopy design? Why did you select these objects? How will knowing about arranging objects in an interesting way help you plan other artworks?

3. What ideas did you choose for your postage stamp designs? Which design is your favorite? Why?

Portfolio Progress

Try Your Hand

4. Describe the ways in which your Expressionist painting is like the work of the German Expressionists.

5. What color scheme did you choose for your photomontage?

Portfolio Project

6. List some of the ways the two pieces of your project are similar and some of the ways they are different.

7. If you were describing your color photocopy to someone who had not seen the finished project, what would you say about the colors?

8. Would this structure fit in with buildings where you live now? Why or why not?

Unit Review

1. Describe the elements of art that are important in the artwork to the right.

2. Which principles of design are important in this work?

3. What medium do you think this artist used?

Teresa, A. J. Martin Elementary. *The Shadow.* Construction paper, 9⅛ by 11⅜ inches.

4. What object do painters sometimes use to support their painting when they work outside or in their studio?

5. What tool do many artists use as a tray for their paints?

6. What do you call an artist who uses a camera?

7. Why might a photographer want to use black-and-white film?

8. Define *photomontage.*

9. What tools might a computer artist use?

10. List some of the things that can be designed by a computer artist.

Many Ways to Express

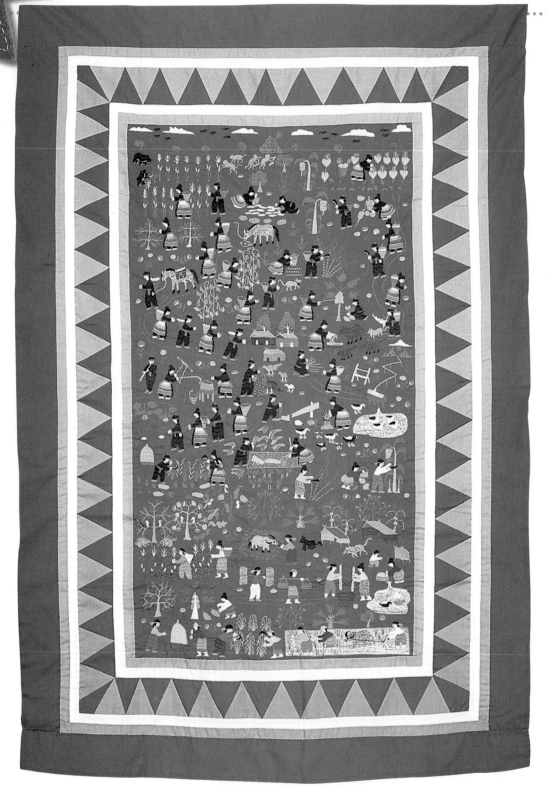

Yang Fang Nhu. *Story Cloth,* 1978 (Hmong). Embroidered on cotton, 55 by 38 inches. Photograph by Michael Monteaux. International Folk Art Foundation Collections at the Museum of International Folk Art, Santa Fe, NM.

Art Everywhere

People everywhere create art. You could travel to many places and discover artworks that tell a story about each place. When you pick up a telephone, you hold a factory-made object that an artist designed. If you watch television, you see special signs, or logos, designed by artists. When you walk through a gateway, you may notice that the gate itself has an artistic design.

What types of artworks would you like to design? This unit gives you ideas about different types of designs and media. Perhaps you'll discover some new ideas to add to your collection.

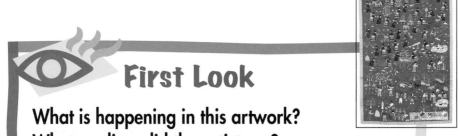

First Look

What is happening in this artwork?
What medium did the artist use?
What are your thoughts about the artwork?

Fiber Art from Many Cultures

Artist unknown. (Detail) *Huipil,* ca. 1950. Cakchiquel Maya people, San Antonio Aguas Calientes, Sacatepequez, Guatemala. Backstrap-woven plain weave with supplementary-weft pattern, silk on cotton, 50 by 14½ inches. Photograph by Michael Monteaux. From the Girard Foundation Collection in the Museum of International Folk Art, a unit of the Museum of New Mexico, Santa Fe, NM.

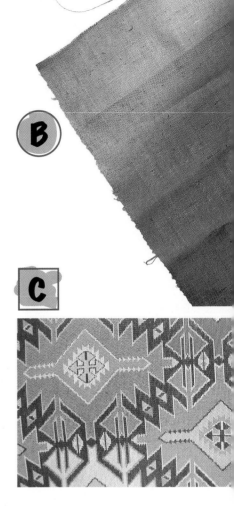

Perhaps you know someone who sews or someone who knits or weaves **fibers. Fiber artists** use fibers such as yarn, grasses, and thread to create. Some fiber artists use needles to sew or knit. Others use a large **loom** to **weave** the fibers over and under.

The **weaving** in **A** was made by an artist in Central America. The artist wove fibers to make patterns of colors and shapes. Which patterns show geometric shapes? Which ones show organic shapes? Who do you suppose wore the garment made from this weaving?

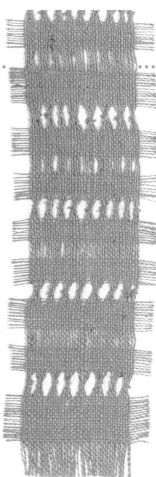

Your clothes are made of **fabrics,** which are made of threads. The threads are woven over and under. Point to different fabrics on these pages. Would you like to wear clothes made from any of them? Explain.

Students worked with burlap fabric in **D** and **E.** In **D,** the artist **embroidered** lines, shapes, and colors with a needle and yarn. In **E,** some horizontal threads were pulled away. Then the vertical threads were tied. This method is called **pulled threadwork.**

Try Your Hand
Working with Fibers

You can work with fabrics in many ways.
1. You could make a pulled threadwork bookmark or an embroidered hatband with burlap.
2. If you'd like to weave a belt or a wall hanging, look on page 146 to show you how.

What other types of fiber art could you make?

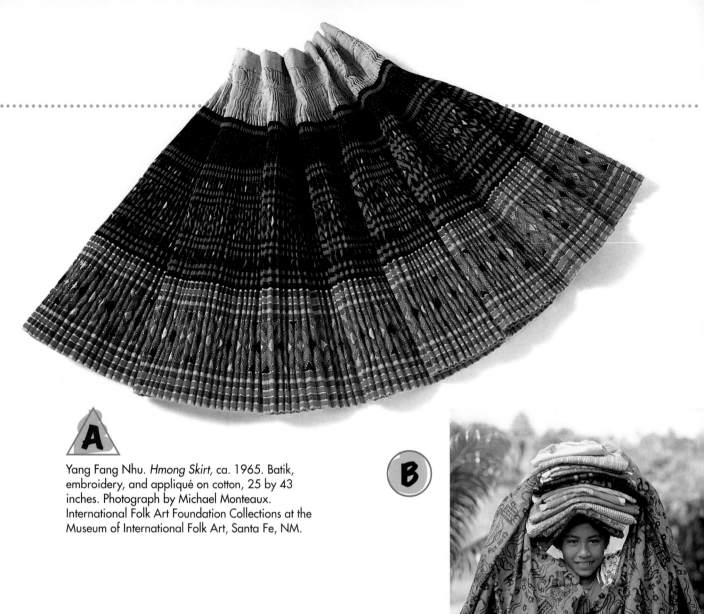

Yang Fang Nhu. *Hmong Skirt,* ca. 1965. Batik, embroidery, and appliqué on cotton, 25 by 43 inches. Photograph by Michael Monteaux. International Folk Art Foundation Collections at the Museum of International Folk Art, Santa Fe, NM.

B

Who Could Resist Batik?

Some artists dye their fabrics to give them colors. The artworks on these pages show fabrics that were dyed. **Dye** is a liquid that stains the fibers of a fabric.

Look closely at the **batik** (bah-TEEK) fabrics in **A** and **B**. The artists made the designs by using dyes and wax. They brushed warm wax on white cloth, and then dipped the cloth in dye. The wax **resisted** the dye, causing it to roll off the waxed parts. Later the wax was taken out of the cloth.

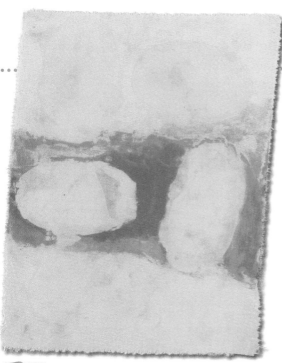

 Veronica, Langford Elementary. *Untitled.*
Fabric, resist medium, tempera, 10¼ by 13¼.

 Kris, Langford Elementary. *Untitled.* Fabric,
resist medium, tempera, 10 by 14 inches.

The artist of **A** decorated the batik fabric with embroidery and **appliqué** (AP-luh-kay). To make the appliqué, she cut out small diamond shapes of cloth and sewed them onto the batik fabric. Point to some shapes in the appliqué.

 Try Your Hand

Making a Batik

1. Fold a small piece of paper and cut a simple stencil from it.
2. Mix a resist medium. It can be a mixture of toothpaste and hand lotion.
3. Place the stencil onto the cloth and brush the resist medium through the stencil. Repeat to create a pleasing pattern.
4. Let it dry. Then brush the whole cloth with tempera paint.
5. Wash your cloth with running water until the resist medium disappears.

How have the tempera-paint stains and resist medium changed your cloth?

Fiber Art from Many Cultures **115**

Many Types of Design

April Greiman. *The Modern Poster*, 1988. Offset lithograph, 39 by 24½ inches. Collection, The Museum of Modern Art, New York. Exhibition Fund. Photograph © 1996 The Museum of Modern Art, New York.

Some artists plan the artwork and lettering for signs in stores and museums, on books and television, and in other places. These artists are called **graphic designers.** *Graphic* comes from similar Greek and Latin words. It refers to sharing ideas by drawing and writing. As you look at **A**, **B**, **C**, and **D**, check to see that each image shows this meaning of *graphic*.

Name some graphic designs in your community. Which signs or posters do you especially like? Why? Which book **illustrations** in your school library do you think are attractive? Explain.

 Chuck Joseph. *School Art News*, 1996. Computerized digital sequence. Courtesy of the artist.

Graphic designers work with many types of tools. Some use pen and ink, while others use brushes and paint. Many graphic designers use a computer as their tool. They design posters, book illustrations, and signs.

For many years, graphic designers have created signs, or logos, for television. Some of those logos are motionless, while others move on the screen. If you watch television, you've probably seen exciting television feature titles like the one in **D**. The movement of the rotating logos is created on computers. It is called **computer-aided animation.**

Would you like a career in graphic design? Explain.

Seeing, Planning, Thinking Like an Artist

Make some sketches of graphic designs to show a message you would like to share.
If you have a computer, experiment with its graphic design tools, too.

A "500" Type Desk Set telephone, 1949.

B Trimline telephone, 1968.

Industrial Design

Look at the telephones in **A** and **B**. What is the same about them? What is different? Notice the dates that show when they were designed.

Think back to the time before you entered first grade. Which new **industrial designs** have you noticed since then? Have objects like telephones, cars, bicycles, radios, or skateboards changed?

Artists called **industrial designers** plan factory-made objects. After the object is designed, it can be made in a factory for many people to buy and use. Industrial designers want the objects they design to be safe, useful, and attractive.

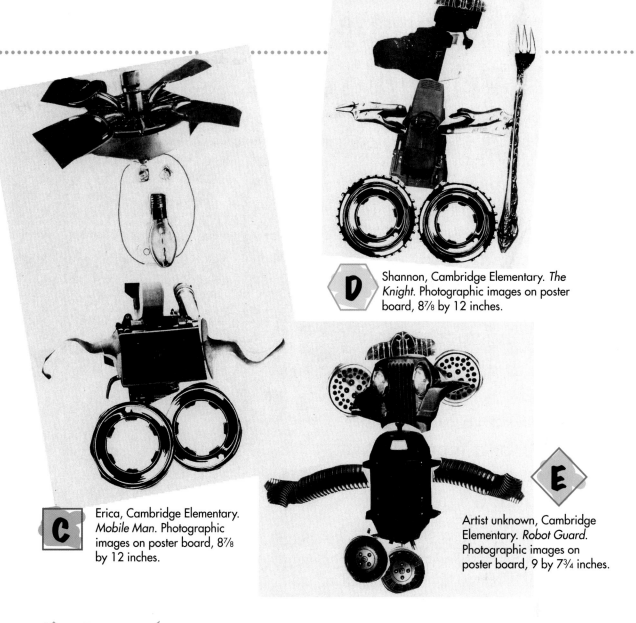

Shannon, Cambridge Elementary. *The Knight.* Photographic images on poster board, 8⅞ by 12 inches.

 Erica, Cambridge Elementary. *Mobile Man.* Photographic images on poster board, 8⅞ by 12 inches.

E Artist unknown, Cambridge Elementary. *Robot Guard.* Photographic images on poster board, 9 by 7¾ inches.

Try Your Hand

Designing a New Object

1. Look through magazines for pictures showing industrial design.
2. Cut out parts of the pictures and arrange them in an imaginative way.
3. Glue the parts onto a piece of poster board. You may want to add more lines and shapes with crayons.
4. Think of a name and a use for your object. Make it safe and attractive.
5. Write a brief paragraph describing your industrial design.

Elements of Art and Principles of Design: A Review

Look back at page 1 to review the names of the elements of art and principles of design. What have you learned about them during your study of art? This lesson may help you recall.

Picture **A** shows an iron grill, or a type of gate, designed by an architect for an elevator. It's about 100 years old. Notice the many patterns of lines and shapes. These patterns are intended to be decorative.

Point to the shapes that look like jacks. What are some other shapes on the grill? How did the architect show emphasis on the grill? Describe the texture of the center of interest. Does the grill seem to have unity? Tell why.

Louis Sullivan. *Elevator Grille*, 1893–1894. Bronze-plated cast iron, 73 by 31 inches. High Museum of Art, Atlanta, Georgia, Virginia Carroll Crawford Collection. 1982.291.

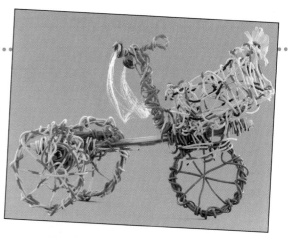

 Melody, Smith Elementary. *Tricycle with Basket.* Colored wire sculpture, 3⅞ by 2⅞ by 2⅝ inches.

Now look at the iron gate in **B**. It's more modern than **A**, and it weighs 1,200 pounds! Notice the variety of lines and shapes. The rhythm they create seems lively and playful. Do you sense the feeling of movement? The iron part of the gate is called positive space. What type of space is between the iron parts?

 Albert Raymond Paley. *Portal Gates,* 1974. Forged steel, brass, copper, and bronze, 90¾ by 72 by 4 inches. Commissioned for the Renwick Gallery. National Museum of American Art, Washington, D. C./Art Resource, New York.

 Try Your Hand

Creating a Wire Sculpture

1. Bend and twist some wire to make the shapes for a special object.
2. Connect the shapes with more wire.
3. Wind and weave more wire to create a feeling of rhythm.

How will you show unity and variety?

Elements of Art and Principles of Design: A Review

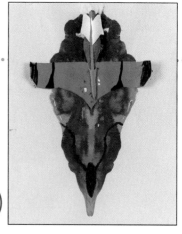

Jordan, Eanes Elementary. *Arrow-head*. Tempera, construction paper, marker on paper, 17 by 22 inches.

A

Lori, Smith Elementary. *Zebra Kitty*. Plaster of paris, tempera, pipe cleaners, construction paper, 8¾ by 10½ inches.

C

Ashley, Eanes Elementary. *The Friendly Visitor*. Tempera, construction paper, marker on paper, 17 by 22 inches.

A Review, Continued

The artworks on these pages can help you complete your review of the elements of art and principles of design. The artists used color in different ways. Point to primary and secondary colors in the artworks. Find examples of contrast between light and dark colors.

How would you describe the balance of these artworks? What can you say about the proportions of the facial features in each picture? Which artworks would you describe as forms?

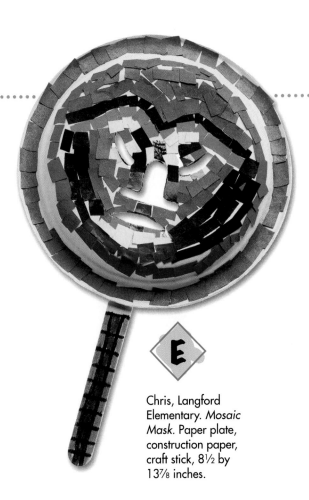

D

E

Artist unknown. *Mask, Possibly of Tlaloc,* ca. 1485–1519. Wood, turquoise, shell, and lignite, 7¹¹/₁₆ by 6⁵/₁₆ by 3⅝ inches. Dallas Museum of Art, The Roberta Coke Camp Fund.

Chris, Langford Elementary. *Mosaic Mask.* Paper plate, construction paper, craft stick, 8½ by 13⅞ inches.

Look closely at the **mask** in **D**, which is about 500 years old. This form was used in community ceremonies. The **surface** of the mask is covered with small pieces of colored stone and shell. These pieces were placed next to each other to create a **mosaic.**

Try Your Hand

Making a Mosaic Mask

1. Cut out facial features from a paper plate.
2. Cut small shapes of colored paper.
3. Glue them onto the face shape, side by side. Begin around the facial features and work outward until the whole mask is covered.
4. Add other details and a craft-stick handle.

Elements of Art and Principles of Design: A Review

ARTIST AT WORK

Yang Fang Nhu

(yahng fahng noo)

Yang Fang Nhu

In this unit you have seen a story cloth. You have also seen a skirt with embroidery and appliqué. The picture on this page shows Yang Fang Nhu, the artist who made these artworks. Her story cloth tells about the Hmong (say *mung*) people. She came to the United States from Laos, a country in Southeast Asia, where many Hmong people live.

Fang Nhu learned her craft from her mother, a weaver. When she was young, the artist liked to watch her mother weave. She thought her mother's movements while weaving were like a dance. Her mother's hands moved quickly over the loom. Her body swayed back and forth, moving against a belt. During this dance, soft cloth formed in the loom.

Fang Nhu learned many lessons at her mother's side. By the time she was 15 years old, she knew how to grow plants from which to make fibers. She knew how to soak the fibers and then spin them to make thread. She knew how to set up the loom. And, of course, she knew how to weave beautiful cloth. Today, she uses the cloth in her works of art.

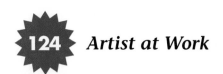

WRITE ABOUT ART

A Word About
Story Cloth

The story cloth shows the Hmong people walking to a new homeland. They are leaving their original home in China and arriving in Southeast Asia. Their culture does not have a written language. Making story cloths with embroidered pictures and symbols is one way they pass along stories to the next generation. What are some other ways?

Write Away

Write a story about one scene from the cloth. Choose a scene from the list to the right or use another scene from the cloth. Before you begin writing—
- think of names for the characters in your story.
- think of a time and a place for your story.
- think of what will happen in your story at the beginning, in the middle, and at the end.

Story Cloth tells a story about the Hmong people. Find these scenes on the cloth:

- women and men picking corn

- a woman carrying water

- monkeys stealing corn

- a man feeding chickens

TALK ABOUT ART

Yang Fang Nhu. (Detail) *Story Cloth*, 1978 (Hmong). Embroidered on cotton, 55 by 38 inches. Photograph by Michael Monteaux. International Folk Art Foundation Collections at the Museum of International Folk Art, Santa Fe, NM.

Look at **A** to answer these questions:

1. What do you see? Describe the people, plants, and animals you see in the story cloth. Point to people wearing black and then to ones wearing bright colors. What kinds of things are the people carrying on their backs?

2. How is the story cloth arranged? What types of lines lead your eye downward on the story cloth? How did the artist show the rhythm of the people moving? How did the artist make things seem near? far away? Explain.

3. What does the story cloth mean? What are the differences between the meanings of the top half and the bottom half of the story cloth? What do you think the artist was saying?

4. What's your opinion? Do you like the way the story cloth in **A** looks? Explain. Have your feelings about this artwork changed since you first saw it? Explain.

 Artist unknown. *Kantha,* late 19th century. Bangladesh. Embroidered cotton on cotton, 77⅝ by 53⅛ inches. Photograph by Michael Monteaux. From the Girard Foundation Collection in the Museum of International Folk Art, a unit of the Museum of New Mexico, Santa Fe, NM.

A Word About

Kantha

A kantha is a type of quilt made in a small country in southern Asia. The quilt is created with layers of worn cloth stitched together and embroidered. Women stitch the soft kanthas often as gifts for their daughters and husbands or to wrap around a baby. The design in the center stands for a lotus flower, a symbol of creative force and life in their culture.

Compare A and B.

How are people, plants, and animals alike in **A** and **B**? How are they different? Compare the borders of the two artworks. Which artwork shows both radial and symmetrical balance?

PORTFOLIO PROJECT

Stitching Your Own Design

In which ways do you express yourself?
What symbol might show your creativity?

1. Sketch a design to include your initials and a symbol for your creativity.

2. Use scissors and a marker to transfer your design to a square of burlap the same size as your sketch.

3. With a large needle and yarn, embroider the lines you've drawn.

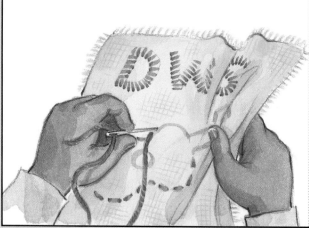

4. Display your fabric art by itself or with others to make a larger artwork.

What story does your design say about you?
How do your friends' artworks differ from yours?
Which symbols could you add next time?

A Vanessa, Langford Elementary. *Untitled.* Burlap, yarn, 4½ by 4½ inches.

B Stacy, Langford Elementary. *Untitled.* Burlap, yarn, 4½ by 4½ inches.

What Have You Learned?

Sketchbook Progress

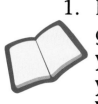

1. How were you like a graphic designer when you planned messages you wanted to share? Which of your messages do you think is best? Explain your answer.

Portfolio Progress

Try Your Hand

2. Describe the steps you used to make your piece of fiber art. Did this fiber artwork cause you to use any math skills? Explain.

3. Make a list of the things you did to make your batik.

4. Write the text for a TV commercial advertising your industrial design.

5. Identify positive and negative space in your wire sculpture.

6. What type of balance did you use in your mosaic mask? Do the colors and shapes you used have special meaning? Explain.

Portfolio Project

7. Describe the types of lines and stitches you used in your stitching design.

8. What colors did you use in your stitching design? Do these colors have special meaning for you? Explain.

9. Write a few sentences to explain the symbol you used to show your creativity.

10. What things do you think are most successful about your project?

Unit Review

Ashley, Boone Elementary.
Rodeo Clown. Dippity dye paper,
crayon, watercolor, 11½ by
17½ inches.

1. List the elements of art. Identify at least four of them in the batik above.

2. List the principles of design. Identify at least three of them in the batik above.

3. Describe how this batik makes you feel.

4. What materials might a fiber artist use?

5. Name the machine a fiber artist might use to weave fibers into fabric.

6. Describe three ways that fiber artists make designs on fabric.

7. List at least five objects designed by industrial designers.

8. Name three things designed by graphic designers.

9. Describe the story cloth you learned about in this unit. What was its meaning?

10. Have your ideas about art in the world around you changed? Explain.

Think Safety

Read these safety rules. Be sure to follow these rules when you create artworks.

1. **Keep art materials away from your face, especially your mouth and eyes.**

2. **Do not breathe chalk dust or art sprays.**

3. **If an art material makes you feel sick, tell your teacher right away.**

4. **Read the labels on art materials. Look for the word nontoxic on labels. This tells you the materials are safe to use.**

5. **Use safety scissors instead of scissors with sharp points. If you use a sharp object, point it away from your body.**

6. **Use only new meat trays and egg cartons.**

7. **Clean up after you finish an artwork. First, wash your hands with soap and water. Then wash tools you want to save, such as paintbrushes. Return art materials to their proper places.**

8. **If you have a problem with any art materials, ask your teacher for help.**

 Can you think of more ways to be safe?

Glossary

abstract (AB-strakt) A style of art that is not realistic. Abstract art usually contains geometric shapes, bold colors, and lines.

analogous colors (uh-NAL-uh-gus) Colors that appear next to each other on the color wheel. Analagous colors have one hue in common. For example, blue, blue-green, and blue-violet all contain blue. Also called related colors.

animation (an-ah-MAY-shun) The art of putting together drawings in a sequence. The pictures are recorded onto film. When the film is run at high speed, the pictures appear to be in motion.

appliqué (AP-li-KAY) An artwork created by sewing small pieces of cloth onto a larger cloth background.

arch A curved shape in a building. An arch can frame a doorway or it can support a wall or ceiling.

architect (AR-kih-tekt) A person who designs buildings and supervises the building process.

architecture (AR-kih-tek-chur) The art and science of designing buildings and other structures.

art criticism (KRIT-uh-siz-um) The process of looking at, thinking about, and judging an artwork.

art history The study of art created in different times and cultures.

assemblage (uh-SEM-blej) A three-dimensional work of art made by joining objects together.

asymmetrical balance (ay-sih-MEH-tri-kul BAL-uns) A type of balance in which the two sides of an artwork look equally important even though they are not alike.

background (BAK-grownd) The part of an artwork that seems the farthest away.

balance The way an artwork is arranged to make different parts seem equally important. Balance is a principle of design.

batik (bah-TEEK) An art form in which dye and wax are used to make pictures or patterns on cloth.

blend To mix or rub colors together.

border A framelike edge around a shape or image.

brayer (BRAY-ur) In printing, a rubber roller used to spread ink over a surface.

brush stroke A line, shape, mark, or texture made with a paintbrush.

camera An instrument used to take photographs.

career A person's job or profession.

carve To cut away parts from a block of wood, stone, or other hard material.

center of interest The part of an artwork that you notice first.

ceramics (sir-AM-iks) The art of making objects from clay and hardening them with fire. Also artworks made by this process.

cityscape (SIT-ee-skayp) Artwork that gives a view of a city.

clay A soft, moist material used to create artworks such as sculpture and pottery.

close-up A very near or close view of something.

coil A rope-like shape that has been rolled from clay or other such material. Pottery and sculpture are often made of coils.

collage (kuh-LAZH) Artwork made by gluing bits of paper, pictures, fabric, or other materials to a flat surface.

color family A group of related colors. For example, warm colors and cool colors are color families.

color scheme (skeem) A plan for combining colors in a work of art.

color wheel Colors arranged in a certain order in the shape of a circle.

complementary (kom-pluh-MEN-ter-ee) **colors** Colors that contrast with one another. Complementary colors are opposite one another on the color wheel.

compose To design or create something by arranging different parts into a whole.

computer-aided animation Animation, or moving pictures, created with the help of a computer.

construct To make something by putting together materials.

contour (KON-toor) The outline of a shape.

contrast The effect of showing the difference between two unlike things, such as a dark color and a light color.

contrasting colors Colors placed opposite one another on the color wheel. Also called complementary colors. For example, orange and blue are contrasting colors.

cool colors The family of colors that includes greens, blues, and violets. Cool colors bring to mind cool things, places, and feelings.

craft An artist's skill in creating things.

crayon etching (EH-ching) A picture made by rubbing wax crayon onto paper and then scratching a design into the wax.

creative (kree-AY-tiv) Having a skill or talent for making things in a new or different way.

credit line The information that is given with a picture of an artwork. A credit line usually tells the artist, title, date, medium, size, and the location of an artwork.

cultural style A style of art that shows something about the culture in which the artist lives.

culture The customs, beliefs, arts, and way of life of a group of people.

decorative (DEK-uh-ruh-tiv) **arts** Handicrafts that result in a beautiful, useful object. Rug and fabric design, furniture-making, and glassblowing are all decorative arts.

design (dee-ZINE) A plan for the arrangement of lines, spaces, colors, shapes, forms, and textures in an artwork. Also, the act of arranging the parts of an artwork.

detail A small part of an artwork.

diagonal (die-AG-uh-nul) A slanted edge or line.

distance The sense of depth or space between objects in an artwork. (See perspective.)

dye A colored liquid used to stain fabric.

easel (EEZ-ul) A stand with three legs, used to hold a painting while an artist works on it.

edge (edj) The outside line of a shape or form.

elements of art The basic parts of an artwork. Line, color, value, shape, texture, form, and space are elements of art.

emphasis (EM-fuh-sis) Importance given to certain objects or areas in an artwork. Color, texture, shape, and size can be used to create emphasis. Emphasis is a principle of design.

engrave (in-GRAVE) To use sharp tools to carve letters or pictures into metal, wood, or other hard surfaces. Also called etching.

enlargement (in-LARJ-ment) A copy of a picture that is larger than the original.

expression (ek-SPRESH-un) A special look that communicates a feeling. A smile is an expression of happiness.

expressive (ek-SPRESS-iv) Showing strong feelings.

exterior (ek-STEER-ee-ur) The outer part of a building or other form.

fabric Cloth made by knitting or weaving threads together.

fiber artist An artist who creates artworks by sewing, weaving, knitting, or stitching fibers together.

fibers The threads that make up yarn, string, fabric, and other such materials.

film A thin strip of material used in a camera. Images are captured on film and then developed into pictures.

fired Hardened by great heat. Clay objects are sometimes fired to make ceramics.

flip book A book in which each page shows a part of an action. When the pages are flipped, the viewer sees an animated sequence.

Folk art Art made by people who have not been trained in art. Folk art usually reflects the artist's culture or tradition.

foreground The part of an artwork that seems nearest.

form A three-dimensional object, such as a cube or a ball. Form is an element of art.

found object Something that an artist finds and uses in an artwork. A scrap of metal or a piece of wood could be a found object.

frame One of many pictures in a filmstrip. Also a decorative border or support for an artwork.

frontal (FRUN-tul) A view of the front side of an object or person.

geometric (jee-oh-MEH-trik) A word describing shapes and forms, such as squares, circles, cubes, and spheres.

German Expressionism (ek-SPRESH-un-iz-um) A style of art developed in Germany in the early 1900s. The German Expressionists used bright, bold colors and expressed feelings in their artworks.

graphic (GRAF-ik) **design** The design of commercial art, such as signs, posters, book jackets, and advertisements.

graphic designer Someone who creates commercial art.

heritage (HAIR-ih-tij) The history, culture, and traditions of a group of people.

horizon line In an artwork, the line where the ground and sky meet.

horizontal (hor-ih-ZON-tul) Moving straight across from side to side rather than up and down. For example, the top edge of a piece of paper is horizontal.

hue (hyoo) Another word for color.

ideal Something in its perfect or most beautiful form.

illusion (ih-LOO-zhun) An image that tricks the eye or seems to be something it is not.

illustration (ih-luh-STRAY-shun) A picture used to help explain something or tell a story.

illustrator An artist who creates pictures for books, magazines, or other printed works.

imagination (ih-maj-ih-NAY-shun) A mental picture of something that may or may not exist.

industrial (in-DUS-tree-ul) **design** The design of objects used or sold in industry, such as telephones and cars.

industrial designer A person who designs objects used or sold in industry.

interior (in-TEER-ee-ur) The inside of a building or another hollow form, such as a box.

interior (in-TEER-ee-ur) **design** The art of planning and creating indoor spaces such as rooms.

intermediate (in-tur-ME-dee-ut) **colors** Colors that are a mixture of a primary and a secondary color. Blue-green, red-orange, and red-violet are examples of intermediate colors.

kiln A very hot oven used to harden a substance such as clay.

landscape (LAND-scayp) A drawing or painting that shows outdoor scenery such as trees, lakes, mountains, and fields.

line A thin mark on a surface created by a tool such as a pen, pencil, or brush. Line is an element of art.

loom A frame or machine used to hold yarn or other fibers for weaving.

mask An artwork made to be placed over a person's face for decoration or disguise.

media (MEE-dee-uh) Materials used to create an artwork, such as clay or paint. The singular of media is medium.

middle ground In an artwork, the part between the foreground and the background.

miniature (MIN-ee-uh-chur) An artwork made in a very small size.

model Someone or something an artist uses as an example when creating an artwork. Also a small copy of something.

monochrome (MON-oh-krome) A color scheme using tints and shades of a single color.

monoprint (MON-oh-print) A print made from a plate that can be used only once.

mood The feeling created in a work of art.

mosaic (moh-ZAY-ik) An artwork made by fitting together small pieces of colored glass, stone, paper, or other materials called tesserae.

motion A sense of movement or action in an artwork.

motion picture An art form in which pictures on a long strip of film are shown rapidly to give a sense of motion.

movement The sense of motion or action created in an artwork. A trend in art is also called a movement.

mural (MYOO-rul) A large artwork, usually a painting, that is created or placed on a wall or ceiling, often in a public place.

museum A place where works of art are cared for and displayed.

negative space The empty space around forms or shapes in an artwork.

neutrals (NOO-truls) A word used for black, white, and tints and shades of gray. (Some artists use tints and shades of brown as neutrals.)

oil paint A paint made from a mixture of colored pigment and special oil.

opaque (oh-PAKE) Not letting light through; the opposite of transparent.

organic (or-GAN-ik) A word describing shapes and forms similar to those in nature.

outline The line that forms the edge of any shape or form. Also called the contour.

overlap To partly or completely cover one shape or form with another.

palette (PAL-it) A flat board on which an artist holds and mixes colors.

pastel (pas-TEL) A crayon made of either chalk or oil.

pattern Repeated colors, lines, shapes, forms, or textures in an artwork. Also, a plan or model to be followed when making something. Pattern is a principle of design.

perspective (per-SPEC-tiv) A way of making a flat artwork look as if it has depth. In a painting, an artist creates perspective by making faraway objects smaller and nearby objects larger.

photograph (FOH-toh-graf) An image made by recording light on film and often printing the image on paper.

photographer (foh-TOG-ruh-fer) Someone who takes photographs using a camera and film.

photography The art of taking pictures with a camera and film.

photomontage (foh-toh-mon-TAZH) An artwork made by combining parts of different photographs.

pinch method A way of shaping a ball of clay into pottery by pinching, pulling, and pressing it with the hands.

portrait (POR-tret) A work of art that shows a person, animal, or group of people, usually focusing on the face.

pose (poze) The way subjects sit or stand while an artist paints portraits of them.

positive space Shapes, forms, or lines that stand out from the background in a work of art.

potter An artist who makes pottery.

potter's wheel A flat, spinning disc used by potters. Potters place soft clay on a spinning wheel and then use their hands to shape the clay into a form.

primary colors The colors from which other colors are made. The primary colors are red, yellow, and blue.

principles of design Guidelines that artists use as they create artworks. Unity, variety, emphasis, balance, proportion, pattern, and rhythm are the principles of design.

print An artwork made by covering a textured object or a carved design with ink and then pressing it onto paper or pressing paper onto it.

printing block A block of wood or other hard material with a design carved into it. To print the design, the block is covered with ink and then paper is pressed onto it.

profile (PRO-file) Something that is seen or shown from the side, such as a side view of a face.

prop In an artwork, an object held or used by the subject.

proportion (pro-POR-shun) The size or placement of something in relation to another thing. Proportion is a principle of design.

pulled threadwork (THRED-work) An artwork created by pulling threads from a piece of fabric in a way that creates a design.

quilt (kwilt) A decorative bedcover. Quilts are made by first sewing together two squares of cloth and stuffing the square with padding. Then squares are stitched together in a certain pattern.

radial (RAY-dee-uhl) **balance** A type of balance in which lines or shapes spread out from a center point.

realistic (ree-uhl-IST-ik) Showing something, such as a person or scene, as it might really look.

related (ree-LAY-ted) **colors** Colors such as yellow, yellow-orange, and orange that are next to each other on the color wheel. Also called analogous colors.

relief (ree-LEEF) **print** A print made by covering a printing block with ink and pressing paper onto the block.

relief sculpture A kind of sculpture that stands out from a flat background.

resist medium (ree-ZIST MEE-dee-um) A material, such as wax, used to protect parts of a surface from paint or dye.

rhythm (RIH-thum) The repeating of elements, such as lines, shapes, or colors, that creates a feeling of visual motion in an artwork. Rhythm is a principle of design.

rubbing An artwork created by placing paper on a raised surface and rubbing the paper with chalk, crayon, or pencil.

sculpture An artwork made by modeling, carving, or joining materials into a three-dimensional form. Clay, wood, stone, and metal are often used to make sculptures.

secondary (SEK-un-der-ee) **color** A color made by mixing two primary colors. The secondary colors are orange, violet, and green.

self-portrait A drawing, painting, photograph, or sculpture that shows a likeness of the artist.

shade A color made by adding black to a hue. For example, adding black to green results in dark green.

Also, a dark value of a color. (See value.)

shading A way of showing gradual changes in lightness or darkness in a drawing or painting. Shading helps make a picture more realistic.

shape A flat area that has clear boundaries, such as a circle or a square. Shape is an element of art.

sketch (skech) A quick drawing. A sketch can be used to explore or plan an artwork.

sketchbook (SKECH-book) A book or pad of paper used for drawing and keeping sketches.

space An empty surface or area. Also, the area surrounding something.

still life An artwork showing an arrangement of objects that cannot move on their own, such as fruit or flowers.

story quilt A quilt showing pictures and words that tell a story. (See quilt.)

studio (STOO-dee-oh) A room or building where an artist creates art.

style An artist's own way of designing and creating art. Or, a technique used by a group of artists in a particular time or culture.

subject A person, animal, object, or scene shown in an artwork.

subtractive (sub-TRAK-tiv) A word describing sculpture that is made by taking away, or subtracting, material from a larger piece or block.

surface The outside layer of a material, an object, or another form.

symbol (SIM-bul) A letter, color, sign, or picture that expresses a larger meaning. For example, a red heart is often used as a symbol for love.

symmetrical (sih-MEH-tri-kul) **balance** A type of balance in which both sides of an artwork look the same or almost the same.

symmetry (SIH-muh-tree) Balance created by making both sides of an artwork the same or almost the same.

tactile (TAK-tul) A texture you can feel with your hands.

technology (tek-NOL-uh-jee) The way human beings use machines and other tools to make or do something.

tempera (TEM-per-uh) **paint** A chalky, water-based paint. Also called poster paint.

texture (TEKS-tyur) The way a surface looks and feels, such as smooth, rough, or bumpy. Texture is an element of art.

three-dimensional (di-MIN-chun-ul) Having height, width, and thickness. Forms are three-dimensional.

tint A color such as pink that is created by mixing a hue with white. Also a light value of a color. (See value.)

tradition (truh-DI-shun) Knowledge, beliefs, and activities handed down from one generation to the next.

unity (YOO-ni-tee) The quality of seeming whole and complete, with all parts looking right together. Unity is a principle of design.

value (VAL-yoo) The lightness or darkness of color. Tints have a light value. Shades have a dark value. Value is an element of art.

variety (vuh-RY-ih-tee) The combination of elements of art, such as line, shape, or color, in an artwork. Variety is a principle of design.

vertical (VUR-ti-kul) Moving up and down rather than side to side. For example, the side edge of a piece of paper is vertical.

videotape (VIH-dee-oh-tape) A film containing a series of pictures. When the pictures are shown at high speed, they give the sense of motion.

visual (VIH-zhoo-ul) **rhythm** In an artwork, rhythm created by repeating elements, such as colors and lines. Visual rhythm might remind a viewer of music or dance rhythm.

warm colors The family of colors that includes reds, yellows, and oranges. Warm colors bring to mind warm things, places, and feelings.

warp In weaving, the vertical threads attached to the top and bottom of a loom.

weaving An artwork made of thread, yarn, or other fibers woven together on a loom.

weft The threads woven back and forth, over and under the warp fibers on a loom.

Guide to Using Art Tools and Media

Look at the pictures and read the instructions to learn more about using art tools and media. Review these pages if you need help when you create artworks.

Drawing with Crayons and Oil Pastels

1. Use the tip of a crayon or an oil pastel to make thin lines.

2. To make thick lines, peel the paper off the crayon or oil pastel. Then draw thick lines with the side. You may want to break the tool in half. This will keep your lines from being too thick.

3. When you use an oil pastel, press down firmly for a bright color. Press lightly for a softer color. Mix colors by putting one on top of another. Or, blend two colors with your fingers. Be sure to wipe the color from your fingers on a tissue before you go back to work.

Using Glue

1. Cover your work area with newspaper. Decide where you want to glue the item before you begin. Move the item around to find just the right spot.

2. Place the item you are gluing face down on the newspaper. Then put a small amount of glue in the center. Too much glue will cause the paper to wrinkle. Spread the glue in several places with your finger or with a glue brush. Spread glue on the edges and the corners.

3. Review where you want to place the item. Carefully lift it and place the glued side onto the surface to which you are gluing it. Lay clean paper on top of the item. Gently rub the paper with the palm of your hand.

Painting

Using a Paintbrush

1. Dip the bristles of your paintbrush into the paint. Push down on the paintbrush for thick lines. Be careful not to spread the bristles. Use the tip for thin lines. Try holding the brush at different angles when you paint. Remember to wear an art smock to keep your clothes clean.

2. Clean your paintbrush every time you switch colors. Dip the brush in water until it is clean. Wipe it on the side of the water container. Blot the brush on a paper towel. Move to your next color.

3. Wash your paintbrush when you have finished painting. Use warm, soapy water. Then rinse it. Blot the paintbrush on a towel. Put the paintbrush into a jar, bristles up.

Mixing Colors with Tempera Paint

1. To mix a tint, put some white paint on your tray. Add a small dot of colored paint and mix the two together. Keep adding very small amounts of color until you get the tint you want.

2. To mix a shade, start with a color. Add a small dot of black paint and mix the two together. Keep adding very small amounts of black until you get the shade you want. Be careful not to use too much black.

3. Try making these colors: Gray—Start with white and add a dot of black. Orange—Start with yellow and add a dot of red. Green—Start with yellow and add a dot of blue. Violet—Start with red and add a dot of blue. Brown—Start with red and add a dot of green. Make tints of orange, green, and brown, too.

Making Prints

1. To make a monoprint, cover a sheet of paper or a hard, slick surface with paint. Use your finger or another tool to draw a design into the paint. Place a sheet of clean paper on top of your design. Smooth it down gently with your hands. Carefully peel the paper off. Let the paint dry.

2. To make a stamp print, cut a shape from material such as cardboard or a clean meat tray. Attach twisted masking tape to the back for a handle. Dip the face of the printing block in paint. Carefully, but firmly, press the block onto a piece of paper. Lift to see the print.

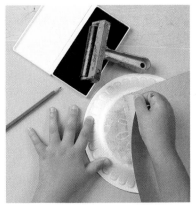

3. To make a relief print, use a pencil to draw a design on material such as a flattened piece of clay or a clean meat tray. Cover a roller, or brayer, with water-based printers' ink. Then roll the ink evenly over your design. Place a clean sheet of paper on top of your design. Rub the paper gently with your hands. Carefully pull the paper off your design. Let the ink dry.

Making a Collage

1. Decide on an idea for your collage. Will it show shape and color? Will it contain photographs? Then collect what you will need. Cut out shapes of colored paper or photographs from old magazines.

2. Select shapes, colors, and pictures that go well together. They might be shapes in warm or cool colors. They might be pictures of related subjects, such as foods, people, or animals.

3. Arrange your cutouts on a piece of construction paper. Move them around until you find an arrangement you like. Be sure you cover all parts of the paper. Glue the cutouts, one at a time, to the background. Use only a small amount of glue or your collage will wrinkle.

Working with Clay: Setting Up

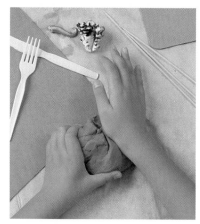

1. Cover your desk or work area with a plastic mat, brown paper, or canvas. Gather the materials you will need:
- a lump of clay
- tools for carving
- found objects for pressing texture and designs into the clay
- a piece of cardboard to put your sculpture on
- a bowl of water

2. Prepare your clay by wedging it. Take a large lump of clay and thump it down on the work surface. Press into it with the palms of your hands. Turn the clay and press into it again. Keep turning and pressing until the clay has no more air bubbles in it.

3. Practice connecting clay parts by scoring them. Press a plastic fork onto the connecting points. Add slip, or water-thinned clay, to stick them together. You may keep slip in the bottom of your water bowl.

Using Found Objects in an Artwork

Be on the lookout for found objects you can use in artworks. They might be objects people throw away, such as cardboard tubes, milk cartons, and old buttons. Or, they might be things people don't use any more: keys, old jewelry, and bolts.

You can also find objects in nature, such as shells, sticks, and rocks. You can put found objects together to make a sculp-

Making a Clay Sculpture

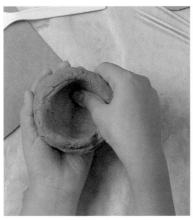

1. Make a clay sculpture by carving. Place a lump of clay on your desk or table. Flatten it with your hand. Use a plastic knife to cut shapes from the clay. Then join the shapes together. You can also carve shapes into the clay. Use drawing tools or found objects to make designs.

2. Make a clay sculpture by pinching. First, make a ball of clay. Roll a lump of clay between your hands. Then press your thumb into the middle of the ball. Pinch it with your fingers. Start pinching at the bottom and then move up and out. Keep turning the ball while you pinch.

3. Make a clay sculpture by coiling. First, make a rope out of clay. Roll a lump of clay back and forth between your hands and the work surface. Start in the middle, then move out toward the edges. Keep rolling until the rope is the size you want it. You can coil the rope into a form. You can stack several ropes and shape them. You can cut coils into pieces and press them onto other clay shapes.

ture. First plan a pleasing arrangement. Then tape and glue the parts together. You can paint your finished sculpture with tempera paint that has been mixed with a small amount of white glue. The glue will help the paint stick to some objects.

• You can make a print using found objects. Dip the face of the object in paint. Then press it onto your paper. Continue with one or more objects until you have made a pleasing design.
• You can create texture and designs on a clay sculpture with found objects. Press an object into the clay and then remove it. Repeat with the same or other objects until you like the way your sculpture looks.

Weaving

1. Make a loom to weave on. Cut a piece of cardboard the size you want your loom to be. Use a ruler to draw lines 1/2 inch from the top and from the bottom. Then make a mark every 1/4 inch or so along the lines. Draw slanted lines from the edge of the cardboard to the marks. Then cut along the slanted lines to make "teeth."

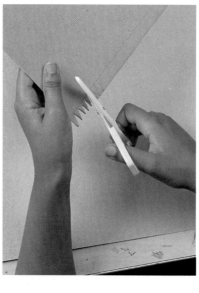

2. First, create a warp. Make a loop in one end of a piece of yarn. Hook the loop around the first "tooth" at the top of the loom.

Stitchery

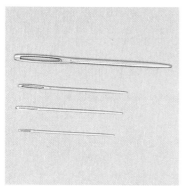

1. Artists use different kinds of needles and threads. A crewel needle is short and has a long eye. It is used for embroidery. A blunt needle is a big needle with a dull point. It can be used for weaving. A darner is a long needle with a big eye. It is used with thick thread like yarn. WARNING: Never use a sharp needle without the help of an adult.

2. To thread a needle, cut off a long piece of thread. Dampen your fingers and pinch the end of the thread together between them. This flattens the thread. Push the flattened end through the eye of the needle and pull it through. Make a knot at the other end to keep the thread from coming through the cloth.

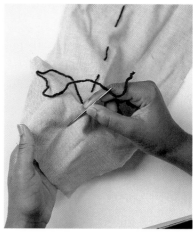

3. Start a stitch on the back of the cloth. Push the needle through. Then pull the thread up until the knot stops it. Continue pushing and pulling the needle until you have finished your stitching. Finally, push the needle and thread through to the back. Make two small stitches next to each other. Push the needle under these two stitches. Pull thread through, knot it, and cut it. ▽

Then take the yarn down to the bottom of the loom. Hook it around the first "tooth" there. Take the yarn back up to the second "tooth" at the top, hook it, and so on. Keep wrapping until the loom is filled with vertical lines of yarn.

3. Next, weave the weft. Tie yarn through a hole in a narrow craftstick. Start at the bottom center of the loom. Weave toward one edge by going over and under the yarn. When you get to the last yarn, loop the craftstick around it and start weaving back in the other direction. Keep weaving, over and under, until the loom is covered. Unhook and remove the weaving from the loom. Tie any loose end pieces.

List of Art and Artists

Unknown Artists

Artists

Index

ACKNOWLEDGMENTS

CONTRIBUTORS

The author and publisher wish to thank the following teachers for their contributions to the development of ideas and procedures for art activities and projects in this series:

Martha Camacho, Wanza Coates, Joan Elder, Kelly Fox, Lisa Fuentes, Maureen Clare Gillis, Karen Johnson, Joan Klasson, Leisa M. Koch, Lara Landers, Tamera S. Moore, Sharon R. Nagy, Teri Evans-Palmer, Julie Pohlmann, Jean Powell, Cynde Riddle, Nancy J. Sass, Lori Schimmel, Melissa St. John, Sue Telle, Susan Urband, Fatima Usrey, Pamela Valentine, Caryl E. Williams

We appreciate the efforts of the following teachers who graciously submitted student art for use in this series:

Wanza Coates, Linda Caitlin, Joan Elder, Kelly Fox, Karen Johnson, Joan Klasson, Dottie Myers, Julie Pohlmann, Jean Powell, Dana Reyna, Nancy J. Sass, Lori Schimmel, Ingrid Sherwood, Melissa St. John, Tammy Suarez, Marie Swope, Sue Telle, Susan Urband, Fatima Usrey, Marilyn Wylie, Jamie Wood

We wish to thank the following teachers for their expertise, wisdom, and wholehearted good will during the field testing of this series:

Judy Abbott, Sammie Gray, Mary Alice Lopez, Robin Maca, Deborah McLouth, Lois Pendley, Dana Reyna, Ingrid Sherwood, Sue Telle, Elaine Wilkens, Marilyn Wylie

We gratefully acknowledge the following schools for allowing us to work with their teachers and students during the development of this series:

Conley Elementary, Aldine Independent School District; Roosevelt Elementary, San Antonio Independent School District; Amelia Earhart Learning Center, Dallas Independent School District; Cedar Creek Elementary, Eanes Independent School District; Smith Elementary, Alief Independent School District; Heflin Elementary, Alief Independent School District; Hill Elementary, Austin Independent School District; Odom Elementary, Austin Independent School District; Brooke Elementary, Austin Independent School District; Campbell Elementary, Austin Independent School District; Zavala Elementary, Austin Independent School District; Langford Elementary, Austin Independent School District; Brentwood Elementary, Austin Independent School District; Burnet Elementary, San Antonio Independent School District; Edgewater Elementary, Anne Arundel County Public Schools; Landis Elementary, Alief Independent School District; Boone Elementary, Alief Independent School District; College of Fine Art, Maryland Institute, Baltimore, Maryland; Orange Grove Elementary, Aldine Independent School District; Klentzman Intermediate School, Alief Independent School District; Forest Trail Elementary, Eanes Independent School District; Teague Middle School, Aldine Independent School District; Bethune Academy, Aldine Independent School District; Martin Elementary, Alief Independent School District; Petrosky Elementary, Alief Independent School District; North Hi Mount Elementary, Fort Worth Independent School District; Cambridge Elementary, Alamo Heights Independent School District; Porter Elementary, Birdville Independent School District; Woodridge Elementary, Alamo Heights Independent School District; Anderson Academy, Aldine Independent School District; Creative Fine Arts Magnet School, San Francisco Unified School District; Wonderland School, San Marcos, Texas; Olsen Park Elementary, Amarillo Independent School District; Liestman Elementary, Alief Independent School District; Hogg Elementary, Dallas Independent School District; Bivins Elementary, Amarillo Independent School District; Tuckahoe Elementary, Arlington Public Schools, Fine Arts Department of North East Independent School District; Fox Hill Elementary, Indianapolis Public Schools.

A special acknowledgment to the founders of the SHARE program in San Antonio, Texas, Pamela Valentine and Sue Telle, who graciously allowed us to share with the world their prized and inspirational student artwork. The SHARE (Students Help Art Reach Everyone) program is a foundation dedicated to students and their art, and develops opportunities for students to interact with and enlighten their community.

A final acknowledgment to Barrett and Kendall, the inspiration behind Portfolios.

PHOTO CREDITS

Key: (t) top, (c) center, (b) bottom, (l) left, (r) right.

UNIT 1. Page 2(tl), 2(cr) Barrett Kendall photo by Andrew Yates; 2(tr), 2(c) Texas Department of Commerce/Tourism; 6(tl) Texas Department of Commerce/Tourism; 6(tr) © Marion Patterson/Photo Researchers, Inc.; 6(cr) © Tony Freeman/PhotoEdit; 10(bl) Barrett Kendall photo by Pun Nio; 10(br) © David Young-Wolff/PhotoEdit.

UNIT 2. Page 24(bl) Barrett Kendall photo by Andrew Yates; 28(tr), 28(cr) Barrett Kendall photos by Andrew Yates.

UNIT 3. Page 47(cl), 47(c), 47(cr) Texas Department of Commerce/Tourism; 47(bl), 47(br) Photos © Robyn M. Turner.

UNIT 4. Page 72 (tr), © 1998 Red Grooms/Artists Rights Society (ARS), New York; 76(T), © Robert Frerck/Woodfin Camp and Associates; 77(t), Russ Kinne/Comstock: Page 78(t) Photo © Robyn M. Turner; 79(t) © Roy Rainford/Robert Harding Picture Library; 92(br) Photo © Robyn M. Turner.

UNIT 5. Page 98(tc) Barrett Kendall photo by Andrew Yates; 102(tr) Photo by Scott Nixon, © 1991 Steinbaum Krauss Gallery.

UNIT 6. Page 112(tr), 112(cr) Barrett Kendall photos by Andrew Yates; 114(cr) © SuperStock, Inc.; 116(tr) © David Young-Wolff/PhotoEdit; 116(cr) © Robert Brenner/PhotoEdit; 118(t), 118(c) Courtesy AT&T Archives; 124(t) Courtesy of Winnie Lambrecht, RI State Council on the Arts.

Pages 141–147, Barrett Kendall photos by Andrew Yates.

© Photodisc, Inc. pages, i-iv background; v, vi, vii, 8(b), 10(tl), 15(b), 23, 24(tl,m), 37(m), 41(t,m), 43(br), 45(t), 59(b), 62(br), 65(br), 67(t), 87(b), 89(r), 93(b), 100(br), 103(b), 109(b), 111(tl), 125(bl), 131(br), 132-152(background paint)

ILLUSTRATION CREDITS

Holly Cooper: 32, 33, 46, 62, 128

David Fischer: 3, 40, 106

Doug Henry: 37

Mike Krone: 7, 18, 23, 34, 84